3 1235 00246 2112

P9-EKJ-716

THE WORLD
OF THE VIKINGS

Ole Klindt-Jensen

Illustrated by Svenolov Ehrén

Robert B. Luce, Inc. Washington - New York

Frontispiece: Helmeted head of a man carved in
elk-horn. In spite of its small size, about 3 cms. from
the determined chin to the tip of the helmet, it is one
of the finest Viking portraits in existence. Found at
Sigtuna. State Historical Museum, Stockholm.

First published by Bokförlaget Forum AB, Stockholm, 1967
Swedish title: Vikingarnas värld
Maps by Olof Landström
English translation by Christopher Gibbs and George Unwin
Produced by International Book Production, Stockholm
Printed in Italy by Amilcare Pizzi S. p. A., Milan, 1970

Library of Congress Catalog Card Number 73-119 528

Contents

Introduction

If ever adventure really existed, it must have been in the time of Haroun-al-Raschid and Leif the Lucky. Of them and their contemporaries stories were told which had enthusiastic listeners. It is natural that the adventures in the Thousand and One Nights and the Nordic sagas have found favour with the whole of mankind.

It was part of the age to play and tell tales. A case in point was the Emperor of western Europe's greatest realm; Charlemagne and his men delighted in hearing tell of the most famous figures of the past, and in comparing themselves to them. Everywhere in that world the itinerant story-teller had an attentive public. Seafarers, like Sinbad, came home from the East with tales of shimmering diamonds as big as pigeon's eggs, of gold beyond measure, dewy grapes the size of plums, and beautiful women. Or else they came, like the Norsemen, from the far West, and lured with rich furs and wild vine.

No more was needed to stir the *wanderlust* of the young. There were countries some few days' journey away where silver riches could be acquired by trade or plunder, and good farms. On an island in the Atlantic green slopes lay waiting, as if for the Norseman to come.

The opportunities for getting on and making profits were limited, however, by the great powers of the time. People such as the Arabs and the Byzantines had special guilds for craftsmen and merchants. These saw to it that they themselves received a significant share of the profit.

The widest rule was that of the Caliph in Baghdad, who lived in a city of a million inhabitants, with prosperity and poverty, the industrious and the idle, libraries and mosques, bazaars, baths, sweet-smelling gardens and soldiers. Under Haroun-al-Raschid there was one language, the same weights, measures and coinage, and a uniform numerical system, from the Indus to the Ebro, and there were no customs barriers here. The Arabs travelled far beyond the bounds of their country and carried on a skilful trade in Europe, India, the Sunda Islands and China. In the East they met alien forms of culture in a high state of development, towns and fine architecture. This was a large and well-organized realm, which also included a city of a million like Hang-Chou, to which foreigners made their way. Here there was much to be learnt. Thus in China they made porcelain and gunpowder (as yet only for fireworks), and books were printed with type on paper. Silk could already be made in western Asia, despite the Chinese ban on the export of silkworms.

To have direct trade links with the orient was obviously an

advantage. Charlemagne sent an envoy with gifts to Haroun-al-Raschid, but although he received such magnificent return gifts as an elephant, silks and carpets, and even a mechanical timepiece, it was clear that the Caliph realised the advantages of controlling the trade himself. A similar attitude was taken by the Emperor of Byzantium, which seems to have recalled the phrase: You shall have the Frank as a friend, but not as a neighbour.

For the Norsemen, large areas of the Mediterranean were closed, therefore, by strong military powers like the Arabs; but in the far south-east, at the mouth of the Volga and to the east of it, where Arab influence was strong, they could have profitable encounters with them. In western Europe the Vikings' opportunities were dependent on the weakness and inactivity in which the kingdoms were quite often sunk. The Atlantic, on the other hand, lay free and open. Here there were tracts of land ready for settling, uninhabited or with only a few local people. Only in the far west, as in America, were there so many Eskimo and Indian tribes that they could offer serious opposition.

To reach so far afield required daring, sometimes lack of consideration, and in any event sufficient people. The first-named requirements the Vikings filled to the full, but in the long run their weakness proved to be that they were relatively few.

But enterprise and love of adventure were only a part of what lay behind the Norsemen's expeditions. There was also want of land. The dales and coastal areas were exploited and populated right up to the north of Norway. From the Swedish territories people had already made their way across the Baltic and founded colonies on the opposite shore. But pressure was also being exerted against the north. Charlemagne's empire was expanding and trying to take in tracts around the northern Elbe and further up. Whereupon the Danish ruler Godfred had not hesitated to hit back by sending fleets to the south which made devastating attacks on the Emperor's allies. Defensive war and conquest were in full swing.

We must not forget that the Norsemen consisted indeed of three peoples, but were split up still further into districts and different groups, socially and in their means of livelihood. One and all sought their own ends abroad. Especially keen to be off were those whose future prospects at home were not very bright, e.g. younger sons whose elder brothers took over the farms. The wish for betterment played a part—the hope of easily-won riches. Only the lowest in society, the slaves, were excluded. But as freedmen, they were on the look-out for opportunities.

Sons of kings and chieftains went off to win power and riches. Sometimes they used their victories—which took concrete form in a strong *hird* and money to pay it with—to gain supremacy in their own country. Like huge, dangerous predators, these seakings were

The Gotland picture-stones and the Bayeux tapestry form the richest pictorial documents that we know from the Viking period. The scenes on the Gotland picture-stones are cut in a very low relief. The prevalent method of making them stand out has been to colour in the background. What we see on a Gotland picture-stone today, therefore, is light figures against a dark background. One of the arguments for this method is that fragments of colour have actually been found in the cut-out parts.

We have elected to take the opposite course. Where the task is to make a picture from a light ground-material, e.g. limestone, a familiar technique, of course, is to colour the whole surface and then cut or scrape out the background, which thereupon assumes the light colour of the limestone. With this in mind, we have employed wood-engraving, because we regard it as a suitable technique for reproducing details from the picture-stones.

The details from the Bayeux tapestry we have preferred to reproduce by a collage technique, in order to convey to the reader something of the textile character of the original.

Upper portion of a Gotland picture-stone from Lärbro, Tängelgårda.

followed with anxious wonder, not only in foreign countries. The sons of the free peasants attached themselves to the most likely to win, and the poets chose those who were specially generous.

We shall look at the Vikings first through the eyes of the foreign peoples. The accounts of their landings and first journeys tell us something of their character. But we must bear in mind that the evidence we hear is not without prejudice. After that we shall form for ourselves an idea of the life and customs of the Norsemen at home, and compare the foreign sources with the Nordic ones.

Under Way

The powerful expansion of the Viking era was made possible by the sailing vessel, the efficient long-ship with cross-sail. In the previous years sure progress had been made in the art of shipbuilding. The new ships were designed and improved so that one could travel on the great ocean. This required a bold and adaptable crew. On his ship the Viking felt at home, as Nigellius—a contemporary of Ansgar—observes. Certainly the master had to exert himself to bring his ship unscathed past reefs, through heavy seas and icy gales, but with the help of his companions he succeeded in the incredible.

Through common experiences and month-long sailing trips the crew came to react instantly and manoeuvre instinctively. They got used to accepting *one* ship-master, the most suitable, and to following him. Even contentious spirits could accept discipline under these hard conditions. In danger they found each other; some entered into foster-brotherhood, and this fellow feeling was an advantage to the Vikings when they stood on a strange shore with other dangers before them.

The ship was the Norseman's great interest. He gave it fanciful

names: *köl-fågeln* 'keel-bird' (flying over the surface of the sea), *fjordens älg* 'fjord-elk' (one imagines the sailor proudly roaring forward like an elk, with its heavy antlers lifted high), *havsgudens svan* 'swan of the sea-god', *havsbocken* 'sea-goat' (butting against the waves), *havshästen* 'sea-horse', and many more. They reveal tenderness and imagination.

It is not surprising therefore that the poet Sigvat Thordsson felt light of heart on that rearing ship with the roar of a lively sea around him:

> Gay it was to fare
> Upon the fiord in storm,
> With a stiff breeze to stretch
> The sail off Strinda's shore;
> The sea-horse ran in glory,
> She planed the brine with her keel,
> We let the ship go bolting
> Away across the sea.

Ship on a Gotland picture-stone from Lillbjärs in Stenkyrka. The two sailors hold lanyards which hang down from loops of rope in the sail. The stem and stern end in a serpent as on the Oseberg ship.

When the poet—through necessity—had to continue on horseback, it is as though he lost some of his elation. The litte quadrupeds could trot well enough along the uneven tracks, but he had to adjust the days' journeys according to their stamina, which was obviously no match for the sea-breezes. Besides, to continue in twilight was fraught with danger:

> In twilight jogs the horse
> In haste for journey's end,
> Hoof-prints lie behind it,
> Where day is running out.
> The dusk upon the hill
> Bears me far from hence,
> Then the stallion in a dusky ditch
> Stumbles; night has met the day.

It was evening when he was forced to hurry past a cluster of cosy farms, where he would have been glad enough to stop:

> The pretty girls are gathered
> Specially to see us,
> As we come riding fast
> Into Ragnvald's town.
> So spur we on our horses,
> That women still within
> May listen in the distance
> To riders, racing for the farm.

It was still not too bad by horse. But without—then he himself had to trot his way through the forest, trackless, as he recalls with a sour smile:

> Thirteen cheerless miles
> Through forest at Eid we trotted.
> The pleasure I can't deny
> Came close to being a trial.
> The Prince's retainers all
> Got sore under foot that day.
> Rapidly we travelled
> With lacerated soles.

It was naturally no easier when later on he was driven away from the farms like a wolf, when he asked for shelter for the night. They were celebrating heathen sacrifices, and were not admitting any Christian strangers.

A ship rounding the promontory at Dingle Bay on the south-west coast of Ireland.

If only he had had skis that winter or, even better, a sledge with swift horses in front; then he would have got on easily. When the ice was set the low sledge, with runners curving up finely at the front, replaced the boat for those who delighted in speed. Then the wide expanses were easy to travel upon. And when the poet's lord, King Olav, went from Russland (Russia) 'westward, first across frozen water right to the sea' we imagine this was done in a sledge. Some very beautiful early Norwegian sledges are known to us from the Oseberg finds. They are richly carved, but their form is simple and appropriate. Similar sledges were also used by the much-travelled Vikings of a later period.

Nevertheless, it was on foot that many had to go, especially when —a wholly peaceful occupation— they had to drive oxen and other animals to or from the market. They followed wide tracks thick with wheel-furrows, made by the creaking wagons loaded with goods. Slowly these merchants had made their way through. They followed the raised back of Jutland southwards to the Elbe, which they crossed by boat. From Nidaros (modern Trondheim) another route wound to the east, curving with the terrain to the Swedish coast, with a crossing to East Bothnia on the other side of the Gulf of Bothnia, or by boat along the coast, to both north and south.

Such tracks laid a sparse network over the countries, which stopped or became indistinct where the wilderness took over, but tried to force a way through marshes and over water-courses. A dam or a bridge was hailed with satisfaction. Thus the pride was justified in the runic inscriptions that commemorated some notable's bridge-building. It also added to his credit with posterity.

The ship was and remained, however, the preferred means of transport. Although travellers had to make their way over land from one water to another, they were prepared to drag their long-ship with them; a laborious undertaking. The Vikings carried their lame keel-bird the length of the Dnieper's rock-strewn rapids, in order to continue so much the happier when the river again became navigable.

Two heavily armed warriors. Detail from a picture-stone from Ardre, Gotland.

Sailing was much quicker than travelling over land, and it did not necessarily mean pulling at oars. The journey from Skåne to Uppland, through settled land and waste, took a whole month. By sea it took five days. The distance by road from Västergötland to Uppland was reckoned to be twenty-three days, a strenuous journey. The Norwegian sea-captain Ottar needed only five days to sail from Skiringssal in south Norway to Hedeby at the bottom of Jutland.

In old accounts distances are sometimes given in this way as so many days' journey, but one must not imagine therefore that this is some exact measure. There are many reasons, namely, why one cannot form any simple estimate of how fast a ship sailed. If the route followed a coast, it might happen, for instance, that the vessel

dropped anchor in the evening. On the open sea, of course, there was nothing to stop the boat—except a calm. In a storm, on the other hand, the ship went off course, was delayed, or fetched up in unknown waters. The speed of the different types of ship must also be taken into account when reckoning the days' journeys. The slim long-ship was used in war; it was a fast sailer, while the sea-boat was roomier and slower, designed as it was for heavier loads, e.g. animals. It had higher sides, so that it could stand up to the blows of the waves and the spume. Merchants and emigrants for their part naturally chose this broad ship, without regard to its slower speed. In order to reckon distance on the basis of days' journeys, therefore, one must have detailed information (as e.g. from the Irish geographer Dicuil in his very complete account of the journey to the Faeroe Islands), otherwise it becomes an indefinite measure.

The Viking and his ship belonged together. On his vessel he was safe and daring. He knew the risks, and he took them. It cannot be denied, however, that many good crews went to the bottom, not

only in battle, but sunk by the treacherous sea, on which nobody could take revenge. So many shipwrecks occurred along the coast of Greenland that we hear tell of a professional corpse-collector, who made regular trips up the coast. Lik-Lodin, 'Corpse-Lodin', he was called. He salvaged 'the human corpses that he found in holes and ravines, to which they had come on ice-floes or from foundered ships.' Survivors raised memorial stones to those who never came home. On his Icelandic farm Egil Skallagrimsson raged impotently against the sea-god, who took his beloved son and let him remain without revenge.

> Of much has Ran
> Robbed me and mine,
> Despoiled am I
> Of him I loved.
> The sea has torn
> My family bond,
> Taken my stay
> Of strength from me.

In winter, ice covered the lakes and fjords and even the sea, inviting journeys by sledge and skis.

One of the sledges from the Oseberg grave is named, after one of the excavators of the site, 'Shetelig's sledge.' The four corner-posts end in naturalistic animal-heads. The sides of the sledge are richly decorated with wood-carvings. On the back one can see geometrical patterns, and on the inside, loops with a strange swing, some of which end in animal-heads seen in profile. Dark colours have brought out the ornamentation. Stylistically this ornamentation belongs around 800 A.D. The Viking Ship House, Bygdöy, Oslo.

When danger threatened in earnest during a trip on that restless sea, one naturally had the gods to turn to for help; but if Ägir and Odin betrayed one's trust, then there was only sorcery to cling to in order to save life and ship. Havamal mentions a troll-song that can rescue a boat at sea, still a storm, and abate the waves.

The experienced and travel-happy ship-master recognised the coastal formations on the horizon and searched out the favourite haunts of the whale and the sea birds' ranges. The above-mentioned Ottar gives King Alfred of England an exact account of how one should manoeuvre on the trip round the North Cape down to the open sea. The strong currents—which are also mentioned in St. Olav's saga about the journey of Karle and Tore Hund—were presumably what one most had to take into account. Ottar will have learnt the incalculable play of hurricane and calm, unfavourable factors for sailing vessels, and he was careful. He recommended that ships going south from Norway should follow the east coast of Jutland. The west coast with its sandy shoals must obviously have been notorious. In a westerly gale boats drifted helplessly on to the shoals. Only at the mouth of the Limfjord was there a free passage.

The crew felt safe with a captain who had knowledge of the stars and tried to determine the ship's position (probably with the help of

a small bearing-dial), and who balanced the length of the day with that of the night. However lonely such a journey might be, there was enough to do to pass the time; stormy weather merely raised the capacity of the brave, as the poet Egil expresses it:

> The storm with hefty blows
> Hews at the stem of the ship,
> Mightily whistling,
> Seething waves.
> Iskall, stuffed with wind,
> Through giant jaws of malice
> Roars around the bows
> With all-destroying crack.

To England

The Viking ships steered in to the English coast without warning. They were met with undisguised surprise: 'Nobody had thought such a voyage was possible', wrote the missionary Alcuin. In the year 793 the chronicler of Lindisfarne recorded: 'On the 8th June Lindisfarne church was laid waste by the heathens. But the following year all perished.' It was something more than a disaster. For the Anglo-Saxons the attack was a blow of fate, a violent lesson from heaven itself. 'During this year great portents appeared over Northumbria and made people sore afraid. There were violent whirlwinds and light manifestations; comets were seen flying through the air. A serious famine followed hard on these signs and shortly after, in the same year, the heathen men cruelly laid waste God's church at Lindisfarne with plunder and slaughter.'

The cry from Lindisfarne set off a squawking cacophony over the British Isles. We know the atmosphere in the monasteries, where the renowned brothers painted terrors for themselves; not without cause. They thought they heard echoes of burnings and the thirst for blood in their isolated cells. Imagination ran wild. There were monks whose thoughts were taken up solely with this subject. In anguish they followed the news of the Vikings' journeys. For the horror-stricken, small bands grew into whole armies, and a couple

During excavations on Holy Island, off the coast of Northumberland, the interesting Lindisfarne Stone was found. In June 793 the monastery at Lindisfarne was visited by Vikings, who attacked and plundered the church. On one side of the stone, the helmeted Vikings advance with their axes and swords on high.

In front is an unarmed man, perhaps a prisoner. On the other side of the stone one sees the antithesis of the wild Norsemen—the powers of good are symbolized by the faithful round the cross, the hands of God, the sun and the moon.

of ships became a fleet. People forgot that for the most part there was peace, and that there were long intervals between attacks.

We have clearer descriptions, such as an eye-witness account from 789: 'In the time when the most pious King Brihtric reigned over the western parts of England . . . there came unexpectedly to the coast a little fleet of three fast ships with Danes, and this was their first visit. When the King's commissioner heard this—he was at a town called Dorchester—he threw himself into the saddle and hurried with some men to the harbour in the belief that they were merchants rather than enemies. Since he wished to show his authority over them, he ordered them to be sent to the King's town, but without further ado he and his companions were killed by them. The official was called Beaduheard.'

One must assume that this incident in south-west England is a direct recollection, so genuine does it seem. Episodes of this sort did occur, but one ought not to believe that they were numerous. The *Anglo-Saxon Chronicle* knows of no destruction of church buildings during the years 835—92, for example. Nevertheless, invasions and conquests did take place. These early attacks follow an amazingly similar pattern. The Vikings—who mostly came from Denmark— sought out level beaches, where they could sail right in with their ships. They had no need of a breakwater or shallow harbour, but preferred a shelving coast for the landing of men and weapons. Thus they were not held up, but could continue straight inland. The boats were of shallow draught, and with the ebb they were no doubt left to lie on their sides on the dry beach. Only at high tide would they float again.

Naturally, the sea-captains had to have a good knowledge of the English coasts, otherwise they would have been unable to find suitable landing places. One such suitable landing-site is on the landward side of Lindisfarne Island, and the same applies to the other well-known invasion points. The Vikings exposed themselves to spears and arrows for as short a time as possible. At the first swishing sound when the keels scraped on the bottom, the warriors leapt out. Not once did beacons—which the Norsemen evidently used themselves—warn the Anglo-Saxons, and if the foreigners got well ashore, they could at once move off against targets for attack further in. Only a few had to stay behind to guard the ships.

The Vikings chose for their headquarters preferably islands near the coast or in rivers. These were also usually surrounded by shallow water. Here they could withdraw after an attack and plundering expedition, and here, on the other hand, it was risky for others to come in with vessels of deeper draught, which got stuck on the shoals. The Vikings themselves in their light vessels slid over bottoms of mud and sand.

The islands—for instance, Thanet, Mersea and Sheppey in the Thames—lay above all in the mouths of the great water-ways. Here they settled down for the winter, protected by their surroundings and their own vigilance and defensive preparations. This is characteristic of the Norsemen, for we see them seek out similar islands for the same purpose on the Continent, not only in France but also far to the east, in Russia.

Towards the middle of the 9th century, the attacks began to be more concentrated. Thus Thanet now played the role of base for a series of military expeditions, and in 866 came an invasion of a far greater size, which was aimed primarily at East Anglia. Under Lodbrok's sons—the best known is Halfdan—the wars were conducted victoriously. They soon procured horses from the farms and moved further north to Northumberland. Here civil war prevailed, a situation which the Vikings always knew how to exploit and which may well have attracted them there. Before the two contesting parties quite knew what had happened they had been conquered by Halfdan. The Danes had thereby gained a foothold—in order to stay. After a visit to London, Halfdan in 874 was occupied in distributing land to his men in Northumberland. Further south, the eastern part of Mercia was placed under Danish rule. The core was made up of the area round the five towns of Lincoln, Derby, Nottingham, Leicester and Stamford, which were all strategic points in the Danish dominion.

Both here and in the York area, the community came to be stamped by Danish customs and Nordic administration and law. Thus arose the special conditions in the Danelaw (the area which was under Danish law). From the towns, which were fortified, help was to be

England during the Viking period. The boundary which was drawn
in about 886, between King Alfred's territory and King Guthrum's,
is marked by a dotted line. The Viking king, who became a
Christian with the name of Athelstan (see his coin, p. 32), ruled
over the land to the north, the Danelaw, with five towns, marked
by squares, and with a Nordic element in the population. The
dotted areas mark places with names of Scandinavian origin. After
Prof. A. H. Smith.

Wheel-cross with interlaced band-pattern from
Middleton in Yorkshire, executed by an Anglo-Saxon
carver in the 10th century. Below it on one side is an
imitation of the typical Viking ribbon-animal in a
very misunderstood form. On the other side, a picture
reproduces the way in which it was customary to
bury a warrior, with full equipment, ready to continue

had for the many Norsemen who settled in the country districts. At
heart they were after all peasants who wanted to devote themselves
to their farming. They found themselves in their element and got on
to a good footing with the native population. The language difference
between the Norsemen and the closely-related Anglo-Saxons was
insignificant.

As soon as the influential warriors had settled down they felt they
had a share in the destiny of their new country. It can hardly have
been easy for the next wave of immigrants; it was not so simple for

his warlike trade. This is therefore a Christian Viking, though one not entirely free from his heathen origin. Instead of burying him with helmet, battle-axe, sword, dagger, shield and spear, they were content to depict these on the stone cross. The old form of burial is obviously undergoing a change.

them to obtain land by a sudden attack. Large areas were under Danish law and collaboration between conquerors and Anglo-Saxons had begun. They were now adapting themselves to a tranquil existence. Hotheads like Halfdan had no place in this development. He was deposed after only a year. The future was shaped by plough, sail and silver-scales.

Among the Anglo-Saxons in the south-west, who had followed the course of events, a more relaxed state of affairs gradually set in. In vain each side had tried to surprise the other by rapid manoeuvres. The new king of Wessex, Alfred, and the Viking ruler, Guthrum, then agreed in about 886 to divide the country between them. In the famous treaty, the southern boundary of the Danelaw was fixed to run along the Thames to the Lea, to follow this to its source, and via Bedford on the Ouse, along the old Roman road, Watling Street, to the north-west. London lay south of this boundary.

A number of Viking weapons have been found in England, but only a few in the graves themselves. Others have been discovered when dredging rivers and tidal waters which the Vikings had sailed and at places where battles may have been fought. Of the grave sites that we know, the largest is at Ingelby in Derbyshire, with character-istic Nordic ornamentation and weapons, with sixty mounds, fifteen of which have been examined. Some of the sites have cremations.

Gradually a change took place in the immigrants' customs. They adapted themselves to the local conditions, and obviously felt at home. At any rate we know of no extensive reprisals when the Anglo-Saxons set about taking possession of the Danelaw in the 10th century.

We have important evidence in the distribution of Scandinavian place-names in England. From these it appears, amongst other things, that the Norsemen were glad to take up uninhabited tracts of land. Thus there is, for instance, a striking concentration of Scandinavian place-names in the uplands of the Danelaw, on the exposed north-western slopes, moreover, where water supply was a problem. The conclusion suggests itself that the best farming land was already under cultivation and could not be acquired. Conditions for the common man were clearly similar. It was certainly not hard for the brave to get into the *hird,* but it was a long way from here to the point where everyone obtained land as reward.

It is undoubtedly in the light of this situation that the following record in the *Anglo-Saxon Chronicle* is to be understood: 'Later in the summer of this year (896) the Danish force divided, in that one part went into East Anglia, and another into Northumbria; and those who had no money procured themselves ships and went to the south straight across the sea to the Seine.' This is an important piece of incidental information. One thinks uneasily of the population of

Lying in the fertile valleys of the English countryside were large farms, which consisted of a dwelling-house and several out-houses, as, for instance, in the plan on the right. Not all immigrants were lucky enough to be able to acquire such productive farm-land. Newly-arrived Norsemen had to look higher up, on the slopes, where it was open to them to settle. Here one had to try to get the most one could out of the hills, where the water was liable to run off after a shower of rain, and where the soil was less fertile. From there the Viking might follow the great farmer's daughter with his eyes, and envy his countrymen who had come earlier or who had managed to marry into prosperity.

Sheep were slaughtered with a well-aimed blow of an axe. What we see in the picture was not necessarily a ram, since both ewes and rams had horns in the original breed of sheep. Detail from the Bayeux tapestry.

the Seine area, who obviously had money and were forced to part with it. But why did the Danish warriors who had money stay behind in the Danelaw? It can hardly be for any other reason than that they wanted to settle among equals, buy land and become resident. Here, it would not do to storm in by force and throw out the inhabitants from farm and land, in order to take possession of these themselves. There were already many Danes living here, who ruled in the land. The area was divided into *Wapentaks,* into districts where free-born men met at the Thing, and where questions were decided by the rattle of weapons (Old Norse *vapnatak,* weapon-clatter). In this way proposals were approved or rejected. It is self-evident that this ordered community would have nothing to do with fighting men; newcomers had to adapt themselves to peaceful habits, to pay for drink, food and clothes—and even land.

The resident population must have looked with alarm on strangers —Anglo-Saxons as well as Norsemen—who forced their way in collectively as a *here*. This word, which is often translated as army, may well have denoted a band of fairly modest proportions. A direct translation undoubtedly helps to make these forces impressive. It would be more correct to use the word force, for as it says in a contemporary document: 'We call up to 7 men thieves and between 7 and 35 a band; above this it is a *here.*' A large *here* thus means a large force, and this might have amounted to only a hundred or so men. When we hear time after time of thousands of warriors in battle, it is a matter of exaggeration. Just to maintain such an army for any length of time, was all but impossible. In reality, the invasion forces in the 9th century, and during most of the 10th, seem to have been unpretentious. They made themselves felt through their mobility under vigorous leaders, an instinctive co-operation as amongst the crew of a ship. Although they had brought no horses with them, they soon procured mounts and ranged far and wide.

It is only during the years around 1000 that real armies make their appearance. Now the Danish king himself arrives, and he obviously had professional soldiers, trained and gathered from the whole of the north. A runestone in Södermanland bears witness to such a man:

'Gryfgård, Endride, the sons, made to father bold. Gudve was in the west in England, geld he divided (i.e. he had a share in the Danegeld). Castles in Saxland he attacked like a man.'

Danegeld was paid for the first time on a large scale in 991, when Olav Tryggvason, the popular Norwegian Viking king, led his people to the Thames. On that occasion they received 10,000 pounds of silver to go away. Soon the Danish king, Sven Forkbeard, was attracted there. The two rulers worked together for a while, but while Olav let himself be bribed into going home to other exploits, Sven came back, ever greedy for silver. If we are to believe contemporary sources, 16,000 pounds of silver were paid in 994, 36,000 pounds in 1007, and 48,000 pounds in 1012. Chieftains and the foremost warriors received their alloted share; others had to be happy enough with trifles. Sven himself at all events acquired vast riches, and in 1013 he also became King of England—this might indeed be equally good: he still levied taxes one way or another. His son Knut (Canute) took over in 1017. He sent warriors back to the north; but, after 1035, under Hardeknut, the unrest grew until a last Viking king, William, who had already acquired his fief in Normandy, made a landing in 1066 on the flat beach near Hastings in the south of England. On these large invasions, there were horses—as we can see in the Bayeux Tapestry—which made it possible for the invaders to begin at once an unexpected and decisive battle.

During this troubled time of conquests, reconquests, personal intrigues and highly charged politics, a final adaption of the immigrants to the Anglo-Saxon tradition took place, but at the same time Nordic features were introduced into the English community. It is in the nature of things that such an influence is considerably harder to discern than wars, which in spite of everything are named and talked about. Danish proper names and place-names, however, became widespread, not only in the Danelaw, but also at other places. We can reckon that prominent Danes became so talked of, even popular, that Anglo-Saxon parents named their children after them. For a time Danish names were in fashion.

Place-names of Danish origin are common. This is not to say that it was always the Danes themselves who created them. If we take as example the name Denby, which refers directly to Danish settlement,

Anglo-Saxon silver disc with geometric and stylised plant ornamentation. Similar examples, some with pictorial representations, are known from England. This fibula was found at Kungsholm in Stockholm. Ca. 8 cms. in diameter. State Historical Museum, Stockholm.

The short side of a stone chest that was discovered in the churchyard of St. Paul's in London. The runic inscription shows that it is Scandinavian work, or at least commissioned by a Norseman. The representation of the great animal and the pear-shaped lobes in the upper corners are in the Ringerike style. It would agree very well if the chest had been made in the time of Canute the Great, when the Vikings held political power. Guildhall Museum, London.

it will rather have been the Danes' Anglo-Saxon neighbours who provided the name. Through the Danes they had become accustomed to using the word 'by' for a close settlement, and it would be more natural for them to name a *by* after the people who lived there, the Danes, than for its inhabitants themselves to characterize their own locality in this way.

Precisely because Danish was so close to Anglo-Saxon that the two peoples could more or less understand each other, we can reckon that the immigrants retained an accent for several generations. Only gradually did they go over to speaking Anglo-Saxon, in a broken form and with the addition of Danish words and phrases. The Danish word 'toft' in place-names was retained after the Viking period and was used to form new names into the Middle Ages. 'Torp', which is the term for a croft, was likewise long in general use. The word has its own special interest through the fact that it shows

the distribution of Danish influence, since it is not known from Norway or areas of Norwegian influence. The effect of the Danes is particularly clear in the place-names that changed form through the characteristic pronunciation of the immigrants. What the Anglo-Saxons called Sheeptown turned, through the mediation of the Danes in Yorkshire, into Skipton; they were unable to pronounce the soft *sh* sound. The word *Scirgerefantun* (the sheriff's town) became Shrewton in Anglo-Saxon Wiltshire, whereas after it had passed over Danish tongues in the Danelaw it became Screveton.

There are other unmistakable Danish elements within the Danelaw; names and little modifications give vivid glimpses of a time when the first immigrants held gesticulating conversations with the Anglo-Saxons, and presumably made them shrug their shoulders slightly at the strange pronunciation.

This did not prevent intimate ties from being formed, however,

The festive banquet begins with the Bishop's blessing, though this hardly seems to bother the participants, who toast each other and exchange comments and glances. On the table one can see knives, plates, fish and bread. In front of the table stands a servant with a napkin and a bowl of water, for hands soiled by food.

between the two peoples, especially in leading circles, who saw an advantage in intermarriage. The immigrants in general also found themselves quite at home in the Anglo-Saxon world, and through their firm social system they came to exercise an influence on English social forms. In return, Christianity soon set its seal on the Norsemen. In 940 the Archbishop of Canterbury, Odo, was a man of Danish family.

While the countryside in the rest of England was characterized by large estates, properties in the Danelaw formed a closer pattern. It appears from The Domesday Book, William the Conqueror's great book of the land, that here the free peasants were particularly numerous. They were called 'sokemen' and made up roughly half the population of Lincolnshire. Only in the extreme north, in Yorkshire, were they few in number. It has been maintained that these 'sokemen'

Two Englishmen, Harald and one of his friends, genuflect before the church at Bosham. It is easy to recognise by its two gable crosses, but is otherwise quite conventionally drawn—it is really more like a chapel. Like all good Englishmen, they have long hair and moustaches. The Normans, on the other hand, had shaven necks in the Continental style. Detail from the Bayeux tapestry.

were descendants of Norsemen. But this cannot have been the case. It would have meant an enormous Danish population in Lincolnshire alone. On the other hand, it was natural for this community, the free peasants, to arise, as the result partly of Viking settlement of these districts, and partly through imitation of these self-determining farm-lands in adjoining areas, perhaps as the outcome of a conscious Danish policy against the landed proprietors. We must reckon that a large proportion of these 'sokemen' were Anglo-Saxons, but the background to this important element in the population was without doubt Nordic.

In other areas, too, in the life of the community the immigrants made their mark. Even several masters of the mint have Nordic names. Minting was an important function, not only from an economic point of view. The silver coins gave the crown a direct income, since the king entrusted the work to a master, who put his name on the coins and paid for the privilege. At the same time, they were used for discreet propaganda. It seems that Halfdan, during the short time he was in London, already had some coins struck. We meet halfpennies here for the first time, and London's monogram artistically executed.

The first actual ruler of the Danelaw, Guthrum, likewise had coins struck, but his Cristian name was used on them, Athelstan. During the 10th century a whole series of new motifs emerge, well-known Viking symbols such as the sword, Thor's hammer, the triangular weather-vane from the Viking ship, the eagle, etc.; and the name on the coin might be as patently Nordic as *Anlaf cunuc* (Olav king). These were coins which were stamped within the Nordic area, and which symbolized the ruler's prerogative. Nobody was to be left in any doubt about who held the power.

If we consider the period from the first landings in about 800 to the century of Canute the Great and William the Conqueror, we find a continual opposition between the written sources on the one hand—with propaganda and horror-stories—and on the other the

Viking coins struck in the Danelaw and in Dublin. The two on the extreme left and obliquely below were struck by Sihtric Caoch ('One-Eye') in York in about 925. Here he calls himself King. On the coin bottom right he is called Ludo. In the middle one can see the coin of Erik Blood-axe from York, about 950, embellished with a Viking sword. The coins to the side of the Viking head were struck in Dublin. Below the coin with the London monogram, second group from the left at the top, is an interesting silver penny struck by Guthrum, presumably in London in about 890, just after he had gone over to Christianity and taken the name of Athelstan, which is used here. The coinforms correspond to the contemporary English ones, but here and there Viking symbols have been added, not only the sword, but also the raven, triangular vane, Thor's hammer, etc. Coins after all were also a means of propaganda.

archaeological finds and the place-names. There are Viking-finds from towns such as York and Lincoln which reveal industrious craftsmen engaged in making combs, and in other peaceful occupations. On a comb from Lincoln stands this fine advertisement, scratched in runes: *Kam godan giardi Thorfastr* (Thorfast made this good comb). The towns received a boost during the Viking period, with its wide connections and lively trade. The unassuming farms lying on inhospitable northern slopes, which the Anglo-Saxons themselves had not brought into cultivation, reveal a similar peaceful expansion.

The English coins that were handed over to the Danes in such large quantities up to about 1000 did not bring in their train a corresponding element in the Danish finds of treasure. One might have expected them inevitably to swell the wealth at home; but not even in the unmelted state do the coins seem to have had any effect on the economy on the other side of the North Sea. It seems as though they were put back into circulation in England, where there was also undoubtedly plenty to be had for money.

Even without the written sources, we would have had some knowledge of the Viking expeditions to England; but we would have received an impression of immigration and peaceful collaboration—and this perhaps, when all is said and done, is nearer the truth than to see the troubled centuries solely as a period of devastation.

The Vikings liked to set up their winter quarters on low islands off the foreign coasts. The wide estuary of the Thames had several such suitable places. Here they could seek refuge with booty and tuck themselves away from the considerably deeper-drawing English ships.

The Scottish Islands

The reckless men who made their way from western Norway out over the Atlantic could discern, after a day's good sailing, the outlines of some rocky islands, which reminded them no little of their homeland. It is true they were barren, and the climate damp and stormy, but they still held an appeal for the Norsemen.

The Shetland Islands, which they called Hjaltland, are surrounded by dangerous reefs and eddies, just as are the Orkneys somewhat further south; but there are also gentler parts, where dry spots provide the opportunity for agriculture. The Orkneys are separated from the Scottish massif only by short, but dangerous currents. West of them lie the Hebrides, the Sudr (Southern) Islands, torn and bare, which like breakwaters take the first gusts and gales from the mighty ocean.

On the islands in the north lived the Picts, who became Christian before the year 600. Still standing as memorials from an older generation are the tower-like *brochs,* often in choice positions with a good view, where it was pleasant to live. Thus later dwellings too are found near such a *broch*. Those who came after sometimes even pulled down the towers and gathered material from them. The language of the Picts was not Indo-European, and through this they were distinct from the population in the parts of Scotland, Ireland and the Isle of Man where the Celts lived, who spoke their own particular language. The peculiar script-signs known as Ogham were in use throughout the area, and typical representations carved in stone show the Pictish style. These contain imaginative patterns, animals—some very

The Vikings were quick to realise that the beach at Jarlshof on the southern tip of the Shetlands was an ideal landing-place for ships. Above the wide strip of beach was a site of habitation, with round houses and on high ground the remains of a *broch,* an older, abandoned defence-tower, from the first centuries A.D. Jarlshof became one of the first goals for landing. Built later at this place was the mediaeval castle to which Sir Walter Scott in his novel *The Pirate* gave the name Jarlshof. The place has since had to keep this fictitious name.

Warriors exchanging spear and sword blows. They protect themselves with round shields. A goddess of fate stands apparently unseen amid the tumult. Detail from a picture-stone from Alskog, Gotland.

strange but well executed—and the people themselves. The Papil Stone shows monks dressed in habits, who are setting forth, some leaning on their staffs. The object of their pilgrimage is a cross: the Christian tendencies are clear.

The houses we know, at any rate the small buildings of the monastery, clustered round the chapel. Sometimes they lie on a little peninsula, protected by an embankment, sometimes on a little island. One such community, hidden from the world around, was on one of the Shetland Islands, St. Ninians. Here, in 1958, under the floor of the church, a rich hoard of treasure was found, hidden under a slab of sandstone with an engraved cross. Twenty-seven articles of silver lay in a larchwood box, including seven little silver bowls, a spoon, a pommel for the hilt of a sword, two horseshoe-like mountings with inscriptions and twelve penannular brooches. Several of these articles were beautifully decorated in typical local style, and the treasures had been hastily concealed from an approaching enemy. This was undoubtedly the Vikings, whose ships with cross-sails were beginning to appear just at this time, around 800. Reports of them

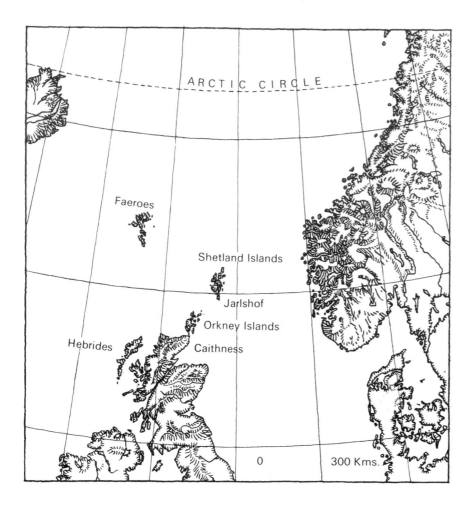

Viking goals in the eastern Atlantic.

The stone from Papil in the Shetlands, right, shows a series of figures, probably monks, going along supported on their crooks. They are dressed in cloaks with hoods and are moving towards the Christian symbol, the cross. The stone is typical of the artistic tradition of the Picts. Ca. 90 cms. wide.

Viking ornaments from Shetland, below. The smaller ring is a finger-ring of gold and comes from Marrister in Whalsay. Like the ring from Oxna, it is of typical Scandinavian form. The penannular brooch of silver is from Gulberwick and represents an indigenous type, which the Vikings took over and developed further. It could be stuck into thick material, e.g. to hold a cloak together. By turning the ring, the pin was kept in place.

The gilded silver clasp, below right, from St. Ninian in the Shetland Islands, is native work. It was part of a hoard of 27 items which had been thrown together and hidden under the floor of the church, presumably for fear of a Viking attack. It was valuable articles of this type that the Vikings were after on their warlike expeditions along the Scottish coasts. Ca. 8 cms. in diameter. National Museum of Antiquities, Edinburgh.

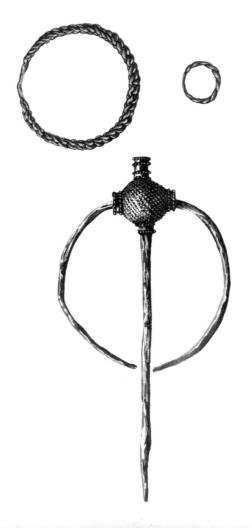

had already got there. One knew what to expect, and acted quickly. But the riches were never recovered. The church was laid waste, and later another was built on its foundations.

The Scottish islands became not merely renowned stopping-off points for Vikings who wanted to go further. Here, others of a more tranquil disposition were content, and settled for good. Nowhere do we get more detailed evidence of the Vikings' life in a foreign country than at the southern tip of the Shetlands, at Jarlshof. The site, the foundations of the houses and the finds together give a glimpse of the Norsemen's way of life and art, and why they chose to live out there.

The southern tip of the Shetlands forms a fork. In the bay between the two long prongs lay the Vikings' settlement, by a flat beach that runs in a curve, sheltered from the wind to both east and west. Here too there was fertile soil and the chance of cattle-breeding and fishing.

The site had been inhabited throughout the Iron Age—man had learnt to make use of its possibilities at an early date. When the Vikings appeared on the water-routes there were also people living in the old round-houses of stone. The Vikings soon saw the advantages of the place. They built their farm-stead as at home, with low stone walls and saddle-roofs, well buttressed against stormy blasts. It came to consist of one long-house and some outbuildings. The walls curved slightly outwards; the masonry itself was constructed of heavy stones in two rows, with a core of earth between them. Similar houses can be seen at the present day in the Scottish islands, chiefly in the Hebrides. There the manner of building in Viking times is carried on, amazingly unchanged. When one bends down to go in through the little door of the house, all idea of time vanishes imperceptibly. The sooty thatched roof arches over the semi-darkness of the room; smoke rises from the open hearth in the middle of the floor, and

makes the eyes smart. This peat-smoke settles in here like a light haze, and billows out when the door is opened. But the room is nice and warm. One is unaware of the wind. Domestic animals can be heard from the other end of the house. They contribute to the warmth and the sense of well-being.

In such a house the Norsemen too once lived. Their hearth was finely paved with stones round a long fire, and in this part of the house there were low benches on which to sit or lie. Along the rows of benches were two rows of posts, which held up the roof. The house—as in later times—was no doubt roofed with straw. Four outhouses belonged with it, including a smithy with a high, paved hearth, and beside it a stone with hammer-marks which had been used as an anvil. One house had evidently been a barn, and another shows a mixture of local and Nordic ways of building. One might imagine that this one (which contained a fireplace, loom-weights, spindle-whorls, etc.) had been inhabited by servants, perhaps captured slaves. In addition, we have precise knowledge of the first Norse settlement through the many finds, vessels, spindle-whorls, etc., of soapstone. Such stone vessels were popular in Norway, but in the Shetlands one could quarry the material oneself, and this had clearly been done about twelve miles north of the settlement. Besides characteristic brooches of bronze and bone with animal heads in the Nordic style, used as adornments, Scottish-Irish brooches and decorated mountings have been found. There were thus contacts over a wide area; that the idea of attack was a familiar one appears from the finds of weapons, such as spear-tips. The dating of this oldest

The bay at Jarlshof was a practical place to put in to for the Viking ships. Here was a lee shore and a level beach to run up on. From the archeological traces of temporary camp-sites and fires, we can see how the bay was used by foreign seafarers who sought shelter and rest here.

The man with the horse is taken from the Bayeux tapestry. The horse is of the small type known today as a Shetland pony.

farm-stead can be made from the finds of typical articles, such as combs and bone pins, which at the top were shaped like an axe. We find ourselves in the first half of the 9th century.

Of most interest, perhaps, are some incised pictures of Viking ships and two men who may be the first colonists. One of them is a splendid-looking young man with beard, moustache and neatly curled hair; the other is a weather-beaten old warrior with a large nose and whiskers, and no teeth apparently—a somewhat battered pioneer it seems.

Gradually as the walls of the first farm-house began to deteriorate they were repaired, but at length this was replaced by another building and then these in their turn by new ones. Generation succeeded generation. Throughout the period agriculture was the chief industry, and throughout the period the traditions were unbroken. It was a sustained cultural heritage.

We know the immigrants through another source, namely their graves. The first generations were heathens, and they received grave-gifts of ornaments, weapons etc., just as at home. The women have a pair of oval brooches on the breast and a third ornament between them. Several sets have been found.

There is, however, one further rich source, which shows the dominant position of the Scandinavians: the numerous Nordic place-names in the Scottish islands. In the Shetlands and the Orkneys this is less surprising, for there the Norse language lived on unchanged right into the 16th and 17th centuries. Only during the following two centuries did it lose ground and so was gradually

A reconstruction of the Viking village at Jarlshof. Visible on the right are the remains of the settlement and *broch* of the original inhabitants. It was from these that the Vikings obtained the main buildingmaterial for their settlement. The houses they constructed here bear a strong resemblance to the type of long-house which we know from Vestland in Norway. The first Viking houses began to be built here in the 9th century. Stone-paved roadways led up to the houses, and between them ran narrow paved pathways, *fé-gata,* for cattle. To the left of the picture one can see pastures for the sheep, enclosed by stones. After J. R. C. Hamilton's excavations.

At Jarlshof figures have been found carved on small slabs of stone. These portraits of two Vikings have been preserved through the ages. On one side of this flat stone is the head of a young man with a beard and curly hair. He seems to be dressed in a garment

forgotten completely. Nevertheless, in 1893—95 a philologist was able to collect more than 10,000 Scandinavian words in the Shetlands. Some were obscure in their meaning, but particularly numerous were the prevailing expressions to do with the sea and the weather. This language, Norn as it was called, shows that the language of the Norsemen completely superseded the original. Its dominant position appears also from the place-names, which suggest, moreover, that

with a high collar. Carved on the other side is the head of an older man. Beside the man one can see something which has been interpreted as a seal or a shark.

the language was most closely related to the Old Norse. The philologist studied the islands so thoroughly that he was able to establish that 'every little hill, promontory, rock, valley, ravine, brook, meadow or patch of cultivated land, etc., has its own name, and these names have, with comparatively few exceptions, been carried on through the generations in the Norn dialect.' Names like *bakki* (hill), *beit* (pasturage), *eng* (meadow), *fjordr* (fjord), *hli* (slope), *holmr* (island), *kumbl* (hummock), *stakkr* (skerry), *steinn* (stone), Thing, *vollr* (ground) are common in the emigrants' homeland. More than 50,000 place-names are known, and in the Orkneys nearly 99 % are of Nordic origin.

To the Hebrides, Celtic islands, the Norsemen migrated in large numbers and soon dominated life there. Of 125 village and farm names, 99 are Norse. It can be concluded that in the late Viking period the population spoke Old Norse. If one follows the river that flows down from the high parts of the Isle of Lewis through rapids to

the green meadowlands, it gleams here and there with bright splashes
and bubbling water. This is the salmon jumping friskily. If one asks
what the river is called, one gets the answer Laxa (salmon). It is like
an echo from a bygone time, when the Celt asked and the Norseman
replied. Old Norse has long since been replaced by the Gaelic.

These islands off the coast of Scotland, with the important outpost
on the Isle of Man, acquired political significance. Here powerful
earls held sway. Here expeditions were planned to the west and south,
and even directed against their homeland, to the great annoyance of
the Norwegian king. After a couple of generations the Norsemen had
become Christian; the bishopric established here, '*episcopus Man et
Sodorensis*', lasted for a long time. We know something about the

The Shetland landscape was magnificent, windswept but attractive to the Norsemen, who came from Scandinavia with its harsh conditions. The Shetland pony of today is related to the small horses of the Viking period. The Viking did not look as heroic on his horse as the rider of today on his thoroughbred, but he was well able to cover the great expanses.

conversion of the Vikings, partly from a strongly embroidered saga about Olav Tryggvason's missionary expeditions, and partly from inscriptions, which are humbler but more reliable. Olav was a soldier of the Lord, we learn from the saga. He considered it his Christian duty to convert his countrymen even if they were abroad. For this purpose he used the Bible, but just as often weapons. In 995 he is supposed to have made an unexpected attack on the Earl of the Orkney Islands, Sigurd the Fat, a powerful ruler over the surrounding areas, who was married to the daughter of the Scottish king, Malcolm. The attack took place in the Bay of Osmondwall, and Olav threatened the Earl and his men with death and destruction if they would not let themselves be baptised. A dramatic and really rather unusual form for a Viking expedition. That the outcome was not wholly convincing appears from the fact that the great Earl fell at Clontarf under his raven standard, which was hardly a Christian symbol. Thus Olav's mission does not seem to have been taken to heart.

But the inscriptions and the graves tell a different story. To judge by them, Christianity had long since been on the advance. Dating from the same period as this strange episode is a beautifully carved stone found in Bressay, with a wheel-cross and figures in Pictish style, and an Ogham inscription. This contains, amongst others, the Scandinavian word *dattrr* (daughter) and the Irish-Scandinavian *crroscc* (cross). Obviously we have here a memorial to a Scandinavian Christian. A similar dating can be made with regard to some Norse battle-axes, which were found in a cemetery. They apparently accompanied their owner to the grave. Similar finds have been made at Christian burial grounds in England and Scotland, and on the Isle of Man. To this must be added that the markedly heathen graves belong to an earlier part of the Viking era, above all the 9th century. Thus the heathen cast of mind was undoubtedly on the way out in the Viking colonies after this time.

There is in fact sufficient evidence that the native, Christian population continued to live alongside the Norsemen (cp. for instance the Bressay stone) or within certain districts. Concerning the latter we are informed through place-names, such as Papaey (Nordic 'monk island'). There is, moreover, a strange set of names on Papa Westray, where there are certainly a lot of Nordic place-names, but not of the earliest type *(býr* and *bólstadr)* so much as forms like *haugr, gjá,* etc. This indicates that the Norsemen left a native population—presumably monks—in peace on their island, and only later took possession of it.

Through their excellent position on the route to Ireland, the Faeroes, Iceland and Greenland, the Scottish islands acquired a lasting importance. Many Vikings stayed out there permanently. Great wealth was amassed: one of the richest finds of treasure is that from Skaill in the Shetlands, which well reflects the position of the island. The ornamentation on the heavy, magnificent brooches is certainly Norse, but it has a special form. This shows that the Viking colonists lived their own life out there and kept their particular style unsullied.

Irish Hermits

Off the rugged Atlantic coast of Ireland one can see a number of rocky little islands. Some rise steeply to a sharp point. Others barely break the surface of the water. But living conditions are alike in this mild climate with rain and fresh vegetation.

These lonely islands were sought out by pious monks, who found here what the hermits of Syria attained in the desert or on the top of a pillar: a place for meditation and self-denial. Here the holy men lived on their islands isolated from each other, sometimes several together, solely for their religion. Nevertheless, it is scarcely remarkable that they felt the burden of their disconsolate surroundings when the weather was gloomy, when the violet-grey clouds sent constant gusts of rain down on to their cold, damp dwellings.

'Fervent lamentations to a cloudy sky, sincere and ardently devout confession, hot floods of tears.

A cold, unquiet bed, like the resting-place of the condemned, a short anxious sleep, cries constant and early . . .

Alone in my little hut, all alone, alone I came into the world, alone I shall leave it.'

But in brighter moments, with a clear view over the sea and milder air, when Ireland herself appeared from out of the haze like a mighty emerald, one received a different impression:

'It is sweet to be in the bosom of an island, on the top of a cliff; so that I can often see the calmness of the sea . . .

So that I can see the glorious flocks of birds over the expanse of the ocean's waters, so that I can see the mighty whales, most wonderful of all wonders.'

Nature for the Irish was a self-evident part of life. It stamped their poetry and received sensitive, vivid expression.

The hermits' little islands became popular places for pilgrimages.

In slender boats of skin people from Ireland came over to attend the open-air services, by the stone cross near the beehive house and the chapel with its slightly curved saddle-roof. Inside was the altar, but there was only room for a few monks.

The Vikings landed on them a few times, probably more out of curiosity than anything, when they were running along the Irish coast in their powerful long-ships. We know from Irish annals that they took a monk with them from Skellig, the high, almost inaccessible islands in the south-west. He protested by refusing to eat.

At other times life was more friendly. On Church Island, off Valencia Island, there was once a settlement for hermits. The island was large enough to feed a few sheep. Otherwise, food was obtained from the abundance of the sea, and gifts were received from pious visitors. Near the beehive house and the chapel was a graveyard—it was safe to rest in this little piece of hallowed ground.

On the near-by island of Beginish were the remains of a larger settlement with similar houses. There a door-lintel was found with some simple runes which testify to the collaboration of a Celt, Lir, and a Norseman, and provide their own peaceful perspective. There, no drama was played out, as it otherwise is when episodes are reproduced in the annals, merely a meeting between two people on a solitary island.

The two peoples stood face to face, and after the first encounters —which may well have been quite harsh—they got to know each other better. There was no need to prolong a tense state of resistance and brutality. Irish and Scandinavian young people got married without hindrance, even if all the relationships were not legally

Church Island, the little island-retreat in a bay on the west coast of Ireland, off Valencia Island. The settlement on the island consisted of a rectangular chapel and a couple of beehive houses for the few monks. In front ot the chapel stood a stone cross with the peculiar Ogham signs, left.

Right, ecclesiastical dress, reconstructed, in the Public Museum, Cork, from pictures in contemporary manuscripts.

The abbot's crozier was the leading spiritual symbol. A sacred crozier such as this was kept in a finely decorated case of the same shape.

The large bell belonged to the priest's equipment and was used at divine service.

sanctioned. A prominent figure like Olav På had an Irish mother, Melkorka, the daughter of King Muircedagh. His father was Höskuld Dalakollsson. The saga concerning them has provided one of the most vivid descriptions of Irish-Nordic life together, and throws light on a problem which has often been discussed: the language difference. It has been thought that want of knowledge of each other's language made understanding impossible. But even if the first Norsemen did not understand very much of the Celtic language, the children still grew up side by side, not only in the mixed marriages, where they naturally got used to the languages of both the mother and the father, but also in the communal settlements, where they played together. Olav På mastered both languages.

Ireland was a large and inviting country for the Norsemen, but they were nevertheless far too few to be able to dominate it. At first the Vikings made swift plundering expeditions, and then settled for preference where there was a natural harbour. They reached Dublin in 836 and fortified the place, which a few years later became a town. The place-names underline the Viking origin of a series of other important harbour-towns: Wicklow *(Vikingaló)*, Wexford *(Veigsfjördr)* and Limerick *(Hlymrekr)*. It is in itself significant that the Norsemen used these well-situated places, and through their energetic labours trade and handicrafts came to flourish.

The Irish themselves depended for the most part on agriculture. The well-provided lived in fortified farms or on artificial islands in lakes. They were divided into clans, and the real power lay with the clan chieftain more than with the king, who in his turn came under one or two over-kings of Ireland. Of kings there were already plenty, and they were seldom in agreement. The Vikings, with their intuitive capacity for playing off opponents against each other, knew how to exploit this.

When the Vikings appeared off the coasts of Ireland in about 800, the population had long since been Christian. On the main island lay rich monasteries; some were famous seats of learning, to which students made their way from other parts of the British Isles and from the Continent. The Church came under the monasteries, and an abbot thus had the dignity of a bishop. The Roman Church took a cool view of this abbots' Church. The two organisations had different ways of reckoning Easter, which in those days was regarded as a vital problem, and oddly enough it was descendants of the town-Vikings who introduced Roman episcopalian priests into this Irish monasticism.

On the first coastal raids, the Vikings were not only after cattle, slaves and other valuable booty; they also showed an interest in

Om Beginish Island in Valencia Harbour, looking out towards Church Island, an Irish settlement which has been excavated by Professor M. J. O'Kelly. There were about ten houses here; some of them are still preserved today, although without roofs, which have been reconstructed here. In the house on the extreme left, the stone depicted on the right formed the inner door-lintel. It bore a runic inscription which runs in translation: 'Lir set up this stone, Manuikl cut the runes.' It is now in the Public Museum in Cork. The carved stone may have been taken from somewhere else in the vicinity to be used for building; presumably it was part of a larger memorial stone.

LIR RISTI STIN THINA MANUIKL RISTI RUN

51

At many places in the British Isles and in Ireland, weapons of Scandinavian type have been found, either in church-yards and heathen burial-grounds or in river-beds. This superbly made iron axe, with its welded-on edge of especially fine material, is in the British Museum, London.

burial-mounds which shocked the Irish. They searched through the great tumuli in the Boyne valley on the hunt for valuables, and at many other places they caused great annoyance by their diligent use of the spade. This is the same kind of grave-plundering as in their homeland, a common practice, as we shall see a little later (p. 215).

Some of the high towers—almost like great factory chimneys—which characterize the Irish landscape were built by the Irish during the Viking period, when they were exposed to attack. They were very suitable protection against the first, rapid assaults, but were naturally unable to withstand a long siege.

The Irish had reason to be surprised at the Vikings' behaviour. Worst of all, of course, was the destruction that went on in the churches, which were plundered of their sacred vessels and books,

Right, detail from the stone cross of Muiredach, Monasterboice, Ireland. In the middle is the meek holy man from Ireland. On either side of him stand two ruthless Vikings, wearing short trousers and armed to the teeth.

The upper part of an abbot's crozier from Aghadoe in Ireland, carved from walrus tusk. It bears the stamp of the latest Viking style, the Urnes, with long, thin animal-loops on the shaft. A fantastic male figure is doing a virtuoso back-bend in the middle of the crook. Ca. 4 cms. high. State Historical Museum, Stockholm.

Part of the famous Irish monastic district of Clonmacnoise by the River Shannon. Here too the Vikings came and surprised the cloistered brethren. The towers here, as at many other places, were erected by the monks as shelters. The entrances to them are 3—5 metres above the ground. One climbed in by a ladder, which was then pulled up; and one also moved from one storey to another with a ladder, which one hauled up behind one.

croziers and reliquaries (objects from here and from Scotland have been found in Norwegian graves). And when the Norsemen had seized power somewhere and settled down for good, they were capable of strange behaviour in the monasteries. Thus Thorgist (whom the Irish called Turgeis) made himself Abbot of Armagh after he had plundered Clonmacnoise itself; there his wife Ota appeared av Abbotess and 'gave oracles from the altar.' She evidently served as priestess in religious ecstasies of a pagan kind.

Ireland's first years under the Vikings' influence were characterized by shifts in the exercise of power on the part of the Norsemen. Under all circumstances the Vikings made themselves felt politically until they suffered the defeat at Clontarf in 1014. But it is only after this that their cultural influence can be seen in earnest. Then Dublin acquired great importance as an *entrepôt* for merchant ships, and then Nordic ornamentation is absorbed into Irish art, which till then had retained its own style.

So it was good advice that the Norwegian notable Brynhjolf gave his somewhat unruly son: 'Go south then to Dublin. That is now the most praiseworthy voyage.' Success lay not only in war, but also in well-conducted trading expeditions, which might well require prowess and resolution.

Ship on the picture-stone from
Smiss in Stenkyrka, Gotland.

The Ship

Although the Viking ship with its outstanding sailing capacity lured
the reckless out to sea, we must admit that large rowing-boats had
done the same for generations. Anglo-Saxons and Jutes raided the
English coasts 400 years earlier. Celtic hermits got right to the
Faeroes and Iceland out in the Atlantic in their slender craft. But
these were sporadic efforts.

The Viking ship was the prerequisite for invasions on a large scale,
sometimes with horses, and for long journeys with provisions for
months. The crew had confidence in their vessel and were aware of
the extraordinary skill of the shipbuilders.

Of all the ships preserved from the Viking period, that from Gokstad in Norway is the best known. The remains of a few other boats
from the graves of prominent Norwegians are so poor that one
cannot form any idea about the type of vessel. The ship from the
Oseberg finds shows a delicate design. It is lower than the Gokstad
ship but was not necessarily less suitable for the open sea. The fore
and after ends are decorated with elegant carvings, which have been
well preserved in the clay.

A few years ago a whole flotilla was salvaged from Roskilde Fjord.
In order to close the passage, five ships from the late Viking period
had been sunk, filled with stones to keep them in position. They have
proved to be extremely well preserved, and although they have not
yet been reconstructed, the parts can at any rate give an idea of the
difference between the types of ship. The dimensions in particular

show that three of them are manifestly merchant and transport vessels, with wide, bulging sides. They were for heavy cargo. The fourth is a slight little ship twelve metres long, presumably intended only for coastal sailing, and with such a light mast-block that the sail-area cannot have been great. The fifth on the other hand is slender and has a low freeboard. It is seventeen metres long and two and a half metres wide, roughly half the width of the merchant vessels. It has places for at least thirty rowers, evidently to enable the ship to make rapid manoeuvres. It was presumably a warship, but it might also have been used as transport for an eminent chieftain.

Of the three that are clearly merchant vessels, one has a deck fore and aft only, and in this respect is like a Swedish boat from the same period that was found in Äskekärr. In this there was plenty of room for cargo amidships. Like the other merchant vessels, it was intended first and foremost for sailing, and one can assume that the crew was

Right, two blocks from the Gokstad ship.

The ship was a favourite motif of the Viking artist. Detail from a picture-stone. Ardre, Gotland.

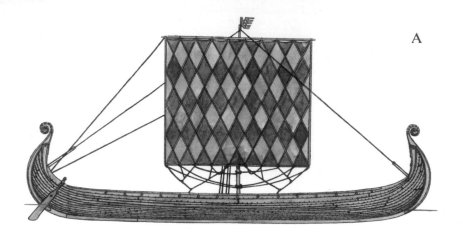

A

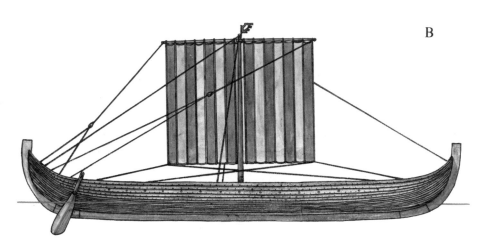

B

C

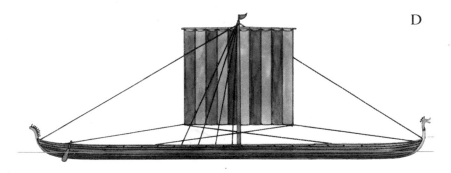

D

E

Outline of the types of Viking ship known up to now.
A. The Oseberg ship is the most elegant, with refined adornment of the stem and stern. 21.58 m. long.

B. The Gokstad ship was heavy, broad and efficient and has long been regarded as the typical Viking ship. But it has gradually turned out that a number of different types of ship were used. 23.3 m. long.
C. One of the small boats from the Gokstad find. A light sailing-vessel, with finely curved and effective lines, formed out of only three wide strakes. 6.5 m. long.

D. The Ladby ship could be reconstructed only with the help of the remains of the woodwork and the rows of nails, which clearly indicated the slender shape of the ship. 21.6 m. long.

E. The knarr from Roskilde, broad and well suited for trading voyages. 12.8 m. long.

not especially large. With its thirteen ribs and three crossbeams, it agrees with the description we have of the east-bound *knarr* in the Gotland Chronicles—a medium-sized vessel suitable for sailing in the Baltic. It is only thirteen metres long.

The second ship from Roskilde was no less than twenty-five metres long, and is thus the longest vessel preserved from Viking times. It can be assumed that its draught was not particularly deep. It has been calculated that the third merchant ship, which was nineteen metres long, had a draught with cargo of about 1—2 metres. These three sea-going ships seem to correspond to the type known as *knarr* in the old sources.

In other respects they have many features in common. The ribs are placed quite close to each other, about 90 cms. apart; on the large boat as close as 70 cms. which lent the structure rigidity. The articulation of parts of the hull gave a certain elasticity.

With the Gokstad ship as starting-point we will go into the details of how such a ship was built, so as to show the supreme skill of the Norsemen in this field. With comparatively simple tools they were able to produce beautiful and seaworthy ships. The large cross-sail is an effective device, as we know through Captain Magnus Andersen (see p. 70), although he used a sail that was too narrow for its height. He still sailed the Gokstad replica with ease in a headwind by tacking.

The elasticity of the hull is the most characteristic feature of the Viking ship. Captain Andersen studied this flexibility in rough weather and noted that the gunwales bulged apart by up to half an inch with the waves, while the side-planking gave even more. Thanks to this particular quality the Viking ship, with its weight of twenty tons, sailed lightly and gracefully.

The hull of the Gokstad ship is 23.33 metres long and 5.25 metres wide. The bottom strakes are attached to the heavy T-shaped keel, which is 17.6 metres long. In this connection we may refer to a type of ship which we know, *inter al.,* from a representation on a rune-stone in Tullstorp in Skåne. In this a sort of cutwater has been fixed both fore and aft. These obviously helped to improve the ship's sailing qualities.

The strakes are laid on nineteen ribs, and the vessel has the same number of cross-beams. Resting on these and held by knee-joints were the planks that made up the board-walk. The lower part of the structure was curious. Here the strakes were nailed together clinker-fashion, but only lashed to the ribs. The planks for these strakes must have been hewn with an axe so that the parts which were to project, and be bored through for lashing, could be saved. With its shallow draught the vessel could simply run up on to a shelving beach. The Vikings were not dependent wholly on harbours, but went in as close to the shore as possible and ran out the gangplank or waded in, if they did not run right up on to the land. Horses could be drawn straight over the gunwales, as can be seen in the Bayeux tapestry (see p. 82).

(see p. 82).

When one considers the construction of the ship, one can get an idea of the carpenter's method. Contemporary pictures, such as representations on the Bayeux tapestry and the picture-stones from Gotland, also contribute to our knowledge of ship-building in Viking times. A good insight into the original technique was gained by those who built a reconstruction of a Viking ship with replicas of the original tools. In addition, we can compare our observations with the old literary sources, so as to get an idea of how the work was organised. The work was apportioned by one particularly skilled specialist. Everything had to be weighed up so that the ship would function well, and this required experience and a sure feeling for proportion.

In order to build a boat one had to have first and foremost a good

The wooden chest, right, was found in the dried-up Lake Mästermyr on Gotland. It contained about 150 tools, and was obviously owned by an itinerant craftsman who worked as smith, joiner, carpenter, and tinker.

Bottom left, a saw, which was presumably used for buckhorn and bone, and a drill, shaped like a spoon. With this one all but 'dug' and gouged out a hole in woodwork. On its top end there will have been a crosspiece. Beside it is a working axe, which was also in the Mästermyr chest, together with, amongst other things, a number of tools essential to a smith, e.g. tongs, hammers, and bits of iron with small holes of different sizes, for drawing wire, chisels and anvil. There is also a curved blade from a plane, which is shown reconstructed on the extreme left. This simple plane was used in the work of reconstructing Viking boats at Moesgård, Århus. It has proved to function equally well along the wood as across the grain. The Mästermyr finds are in the State Historical Museum, Stockholm.

Shipbuilding as depicted in the Bayeux tapestry. Trees are
felled, and the logs split with the broad-bladed axe. The hull is
being constructed and holes are being bored for the nails.

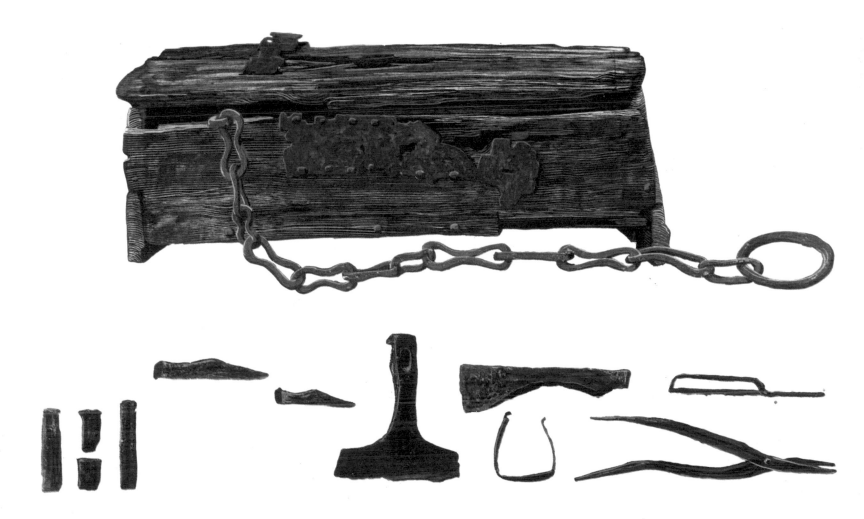

A strong triangular panel fills out the inside of the prow of the Oseberg ship. It is decorated with most striking motifs—clutching beasts, some all but human. They cling tight to each other or to their long beards and their own feet. They were done by the same artist who carved the stem and stern of the ship, a skilful and imaginative master.

Two oars from the Oseberg grave. The Viking Ship House, Bygdöy, Oslo.

Dragon-head, drawn from a fragment of a mould found at Birka. State Historical Museum, Stockholm.

supply of suitable wood, oak if possible, at least for the more important parts. The keel had to be made from a single piece in order to be durable, with smaller pieces only let in fore and aft to lead on to the end-posts. The keel gave the ship stability and together with the strakes at deck-level a certain stiffness. That long-ships were constructed with keels made up of more than one piece — as is related in the later sagas — is thus not very likely.

Later on, when ships were built with rigid hulls and the strakes nailed to the ribs, it would be more probable. It is understandable, therefore, that Viking ships over twenty-five metres long have not been found.

Oak was the predominant material. It is hard and can be split radially. There was less waste of wood that way than with parallel cutting, where only two planks could be got from one trunk. Each plank or keel could be hewn with the broad-bladed axe by wedging one end of the piece of wood into the fork of a tree — as appears from the Bayeux tapestry. The carpenter must have had a knack with his axe, just as the carver had with his knife. The planks had to be of different thicknesses. In the Gokstad ship the bottom strakes and the upper planking measure only 2.6 cms., while the planks at the waterline were made thicker, 4.4 cms. The thole-board, through which the oars passed, was also substantial, while the uppermost strake just under the gunwales was only 1.6 cms. thick. To trim the planks a simple plane was used, which consisted of a blade across the end of a short, thick shaft.

When the carpenter was ready, the next specialist, the stem-maker, could begin. He had the responsible job of hewing the keel and the end-posts. The ends were given their elegant curve, and it might happen that they were decorated with carvings. In such a case the stem-maker would undoubtedly hand the work over to a wood-carver. The ornaments which crowned the ends were detachable and not used on all ships. On the Bayeux tapestry several ships can be seen lying without dragon-heads, and in the Icelandic Ulfljot chronicle we receive a rather fanciful explanation: one ought not to sail across the sea (from abroad) in ships adorned with dragon-heads. But if one did, one should remove the heads before land came

These pieces of wood, which were found with shreds of ropework, come from Norwegian ship-graves. Left, a block from Gokstad; the use for which it was intended was illustrated on p. 58. The other pieces come from Oseberg and one can assume that they belonged to the vessels' rigging. Cp. the picture of the Gotland sailors p. 68.

into sight, and not sail into the shore with the gaping heads, thus frightening the spirits of the land.

The shipwright, the master shipbuilder, followed the work closely. He was familiar with the consequences involved in each alteration, good as well as risky. There is an amusing story about a shipwright who for a short time was away from the work. The craftsmen took the opportunity to alter the form of the ship according to what they considered best. But when he came home again, he continued alone and in brooding silence, and with his axe restored the boat to the design he had conceived. And it actually was—to his assistants' surprise—a successful ship.

The planks were fixed to the keel and the end-posts, and the ribs added. At the same time, the seams were caulked with animal-hair dipped in tar. The mast is reckoned to have been about twelve metres high (only a part of the mast was preserved in the Gokstad grave). We must remember that the pressure from the large cross-sail was

Right, the 'mast-fish' seen from the side in section at the rib just aft of the mast. Below on the keel lies a heavy block of oak, the 'old woman', with a hole for the mast. The mast-fish itself is a block of oak with an open slit at the back so that the mast can be lowered. When the mast is raised it is locked tight with a wedge. To be seen in the planking are the shutters that cover the oar-holes.

Shipbuilders at work. Most of the planks were nailed
before the ribs were pressed down into the hull and
stretched out. After that the upper planks were laid
on. The ship was made tight with tow dipped in
boiling tar. The joining of the planks was done with
iron clinch nails.

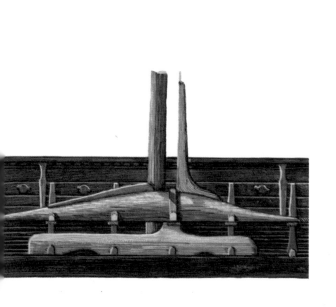

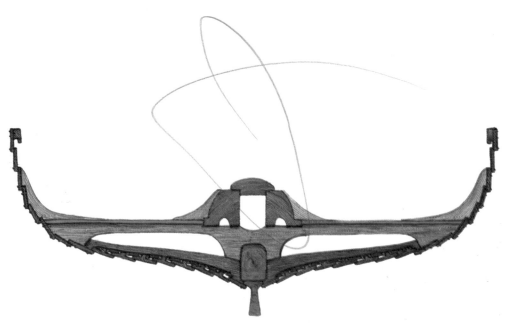

Sail-setting, left, for running before the wind; centre, for reaching; right, for sailing close to the wind. In the left-hand picture, the sail is stretched out at the bottom by two booms. In the centre picture, the sail is stretched forward by one boom. In the right-hand picture, the fore bolt-rope, i.e. one of the ropes that edge the sail, is stretched by a line to a boom that sticks out over the prow.

Below: Detail from a picture-stone from Smiss in Stenkyrka, Gotland. Note that the crew hold on to loops from the sail. It is possible that the wooden pegs, p. 66, nos. 2 and 3 from the left, were intended for rope-ends such as these.

very great. This appears from the solid base for the mast. To secure it, there were two fixing-points: next to the keel, an oak block 3.6 metres long, 'the old woman', which distributed the thrust of the mast to the keel and the ribs, and which had a hole in the middle where the mast stood. Above this, on the cross-beams lay 'the mast-fish', a long baulk of timber, the fore part of which was solid while the after part had a slit so that the mast could be lowered. When the mast was up, this was closed with a bolt and braced against the sides of the ship with two further baulks. Presumably there were also stays from the mast-top to the stem-post.

The cross-beams supported a flat deck of loose planks. Beneath these was a cavity, not particularly deep, where any cargo might lie protected and also help to stabilize the boat.

The sail, with an area of 90 square metres, was bent on a yard which was roughly 11.5 metres long. At the very top of the mast, as a proud ensign, was a triangular weather-vane of gilded bronze. Several of these have been preserved (though not from the Gokstad ship), all from a rather late period and decorated with magnificent animal-figures.

On the deck of the Gokstad boat are two blocks of wood, one on either side, each with two holes to receive booms eight metres long. These seem to have held the lower corners of the sail out-stretched. The booms were placed in the rear holes when they were to hold the opposite corners of the sail taut. The front hole in the two blocks may

have received a boom which held the sail obliquely and caught the wind from the side. This boom thus secured the front corner of the lower edge of the sail, so that it was held firm. In this way they could make do with one supporting yard and had no need of a lower one to keep the sail stretched.

A simple arrangement for reefing was no less important for the ship's manoeuvrability. On the picture-stones from Gotland we can see where rope-ends, tied together, hang down from the sail. The crew hold on to them, perhaps by little pegs like those from the Gokstad find. At all events the great sail had to be very strong, and so it was reinforced with ropes or thongs in a diamond pattern. In the Gokstad grave there was a heavy piece of coarse woollen cloth, which may have been the sail. It consisted of wide strips sewn together, white alternating with another colour.

Although the Viking ships were propelled first and foremost by the wind, they were easy to row. The oars of the Gokstad ship measured from 5.3 to 5.85 metres. The longest were used next to the ends of the boat, where the strakes with the oar-holes were higher and where the boat narrowed. The distance between oar-holes and waterline was barely half a metre. Between the holes it is 95 cms. Presumably they rowed with short strokes, just as one can see today at the Olai Regatta in the Faeroe Islands. This technique is practical, moreover, in heavy seas and for long periods of rowing. The rowers sat quite close together, therefore, no doubt on low seamen's chests in which they kept their private belongings.

The 32 holes for the oars were made as small as possible so that splashes from the waves should not penetrate. When the oars were not in use, the holes were stopped up with bungs of wood or hide.

The rudder, 3.3 metres long, is of oak and has the same shape as an oar, only much broader. Near the top it is furnished with a crosspiece, the actual tiller. The whole is lashed with withies to a block near the stern on the starboard side. It can be swivelled both horizontally and vertically. When the boat ran into shallow water, the rudder had to be raised, since it projected half a metre below the keel. This was done with the help of a rope fastened to a hole in the bottom end of the rudder.

The rudder from one of the small boats in the Gokstad find. The rudders of the large ships were of the same shape only bigger.

On the Gokstad ships, there was only one little touch of ornamental decoration, but of high quality. This is the tiller, which is finely carved with a gaping animal-head. The Viking Ship House, Bygdöy, Oslo.

We know how effective this side-rudder was and in general how excellently the Viking ship acquitted herself on the open sea. As already mentioned, Captain Magnus Andersen has given an account of his journey across the Atlantic in a replica of the Gokstad ship. He was particularly interested in the rudder, as he distrusted it at first. This attitude turned to admiration, however, after the first few days' sailing, and he never had to use the stern-rudder which he had in reserve. He thus had the chance to test the side-rudder in all sorts of weather and different wind directions. He had to acknowledge that it was unusually suitable for a boat of this type. It worked very simply—it was enough to have one man at the helm even in rough weather.

The Gokstad ship with its 32 oar-holes can be described as a 16-seater. When we read in the Anglo-Saxon Chronicle that King Alfred built ships 'nearly twice as big as the others,' we can assume that they were of a different type—which the Chronicle also underlines through

the fact that neither a Danish nor a Frisian model was used. They were men-of-war, higher and with a deeper draught than the ships of the Vikings.

It is hard to believe at first that the Viking ships were suitable for sea-battles, and yet nearly all the decisive trials of strength of the time were fought at sea. The crew, who had only their shields to protect them, were undeniably vulnerable to arrows and spears, not to mention stones. The prevailing mode of fighting, when it came to close combat, oddly enough was to lash the ships together, one after the other, so that they lay like a vast floating fortress, with the warriors ready to board the enemy in several ranks. Then there was room to take up a position and use, not only throwing weapons, but also swords, clubs and shields. To jump right in among one's opponents and cause confusion was a highly-regarded exploit. In return it was a favourite trick of the opponents to hack at the sides of these great floating castles and detach the outer ships from the rest.

Emigrants across the Atlantic

None of the Vikings' exploits has made a greater impression on posterity than their voyage to Greenland and America. They had already ventured out across the great oceans and laid claim to large tracts of virgin land in Iceland and the Faeroes. To these they came from west Norway, the Scottish islands or Ireland, to places that were already inhabited—here were Celtic monks who sought sanctuary on deserted islands. The Norsemen came in a different way, with animals and household goods, and divided the land between them. They originated from the greater part of Scandinavia, most often Norway, and had with them Celtic retainers, which explains the characteristic strain in the Icelandic population. It was slaves and their wives who helped to give life in the new community its character. One of the pioneers, a prominent farmer with his house-carls, was Skallagrim, who took land at Borgarfjord. He was skilled at many crafts, such as smithing and shipbuilding, and understood agriculture and fishing. 'He always kept a band of men at hand, and sought eagerly after such necessaries as might be found in the district and which might be of use to them; for at first they had too few cattle compared to what was needed for the large number of men. What livestock they possessed, however, had to look for its own food in the forest throughout the winter. Skallagrim was a good shipbuilder, and there was no lack of driftwood on the coast west of

the marshes. He had a farm built at Alptanäs, and had a second home there. From there he ordered his men to go out in rowing-boats to fish, hunt seals and collect eggs, for there was an ample supply of all those, and likewise of driftwood to take home. At that time whales were often stranded, and there was liberty for all to harpoon them. And wild animals in those days lay still and at ease in the hunting grounds, for men were unknown to them.'

Life was full of opportunities for the industrious who wanted to procure a living. Here there was room for sheep-farming amongst other things. Iceland became, just like the Faeroes, part of the North, on a par with the barren parts of northern Norway.

From the islands in the Atlantic, the Norsemen made their way further, and found land far to the west. Shortly after 900, an Icelander, Gunbjörn, was thrown off course on his way home from Norway. At length he saw a new land with out-lying islands, which must have been the Greenland coast near Angmagssalik. The discovery did not acquire importance, however, until later generations.

Erik the Red, a fiery Norseman, was banished from his homeland in the 960s, and sailed to Iceland with his father Torvald. There he married Thjodhild, and through her received good land at Breidafjord. But as a consequence of his violent disposition his life took yet another turn: in 982 he was banished for three years. He went off with his men to search for the regions that Gunbjörn had glimpsed; he rediscovered the land, sailed along it and studied it carefully. After the three years had passed he headed back to Iceland. Then, to arouse the interest of his fellow countrymen, he called the island Greenland, and invited them to go there with him. It is related that

thirty-five ships with colonists put out to sea, but only fourteen got there. The rest were driven back or perished. For himself, he chose Brattahlid in Eriksfjord, a piece of lush meadowland below the mountains, while the others spread themselves out with their animals and household goods, over the habitable areas of south-west Greenland, partly in the south, where the majority took land (Österbygden, 'the eastern settlement'), and partly further north (Västerbygden, 'the western settlement').

Erik the Red became the uncrowned ruler there. 'Everybody went by what he said, and this lasted as long as he lived.' The power was later shared between the large farmers, but to begin with he dominated everything with his somewhat testy nature. He worshipped the Nordic gods and shunned Christianity. And when his son Leif, who did not take after him in temperament, had himself baptized in Norway, the skirmishings began. Leif had a priest with him for Greenland, and on his way back he rescued some castaways. He had a mixed reception from his parents. Erik declared that 'one thing

Brattahlid, the farmstead which Erik the Red built from the beginning in a suitable and magnificent landscape. It was extended and received additions. The strangest of them is undoubtedly the little turf church which can be seen slightly right of centre in

74

the drawing, and below in a close view. It was placed a certain distance from the farm so that it should not annoy Erik, who after all was not a Christian. The church was no bigger than the little chapels in Ireland and Scotland, and could only hold a few people.

might make up for the other: that he had saved a ship's crew in distress, and that he had brought the obnoxious person to Greenland.' By 'obnoxious person' he meant the priest.

In a saga about it, the *Haugsbok,* we learn what happened afterwards: 'Erik was slow to come to any decision about giving up his faith, but Thjodhild soon let herself be persuaded, and she had a church built a short distance from the houses; this building was called Thjodhild's church. There, she and the others who had gone over to Christianity held their prayers. From the moment she adopted the faith, Thjodhild would not share her bed with Erik; and this was much against his wishes.' He can hardly have looked upon the church with a benevolent eye.

We know the outward setting for these events. The church has been excavated. It is a very small, square turf-building, which recalls most of all the Celtic chapels on the Scottish islands and in Ireland. The interior measures only two metres by four, with wooden panels and a saddle-roof supported by posts. It was surrounded by a

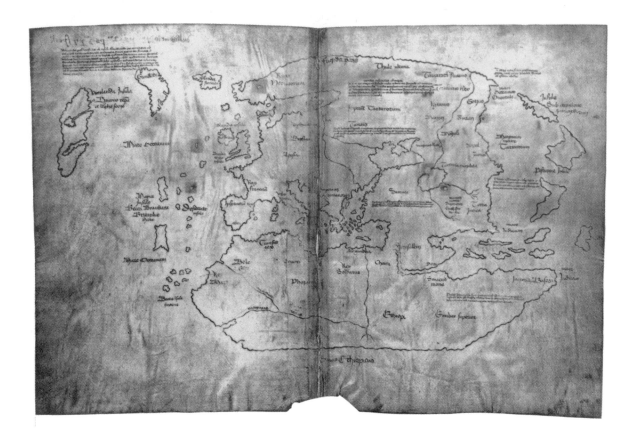

cemetery. One cannot avoid the thought that Erik may have found his last resting-place here, in spite of everything.

Brattahlid consisted of a series of rooms built together, with thick, snug walls of stone and turf. Here there was plenty of room for people and animals. In the middle of the floor blazed the long fire. Whether the farmhouse was already so extensive from the beginning, in Erik's time, is an open question. The farms in Greenland, namely, gradually came to be built round a passage with which the rooms connected. One entered by the side and end rooms with sleeping quarters, kitchen, bathroom, living-room, etc. In this way the heat could be kept in. This was naturally a problem in the arctic climate. Another was keeping the domestic animals alive through the winter. This required a large store of hay. That corn did not grow well was known to the other Norsemen, who heard tell of conditions from returning travellers. 'It is said that there are large pasture-lands in

The recently discovered map of the world which it is thought can be dated to the time before Columbus. The outermost parts on the left and right, with America and China, are otherwise unknown in maps from the Middle Ages. The details of America in this case can only be derived from the accounts of the Vikings, which also appears from the text: 'The island of Vinland, found by the companions Bjarne and Leif.' The coastline agrees well with the area near Newfoundland and the stretches to the north. University Library, Yale, U. S. A.

Reconstruction of a bearing-dial after sketches by Carl V. Sølver. It is built up from the fragment right, which was found at 'The Nunnery' in Unartoq Fjord in Österbygden, Greenland. The instrument was used, with the help of the sun and the shadow cast by the pin on the dial, to determine one's course, which could then be marked with the horizontal course-pointer. Ca. 7 cms. in diameter. National Museum, Copenhagen.

Below, Viking ships slipping out of Herjolfsnes in Österbygden, Greenland.

Greenland and that there are large and fine farms, for there they have a lot of cattle and sheep, so that much butter and cheese is made. The people live on these for the most part, and also on meat from all kinds of game, such as the meat of reindeer, whale, seal and bear.'

In the summer of 986, the Icelander Bjarne sailed home from Norway with his ship fully loaded in order to spend the winter with his father Herjolf. When he arrived he found that during his absence his father had emigrated to Greenland. So, with his comrades' agreement, he followed. But a violent gale from the north sprang up and drove them, after many days' helpless drifting, in towards a landscape with hills and forests. It could not be Greenland. They sheered off to the north and held the same course for two days, along wooded lowlands. After sailing for a further two days, they caught sight of mountain ranges with glaciers. Here, they changed course to the east, and after four days' journey reached Herjolfsnes in Greenland.

This adventure was much talked about in the Greenland settlements, and Erik the Red and his sons received the urge to make the journey. Erik happened to fall off his horse on the way to the ship, which they had bought from Bjarne. He broke several bones, a bad omen; but in spite of this Leif decided to make the journey alone. He went back along Bjarne's traces and came first to the land Bjarne had found last. He called the three regions, after Bjarne's description, Helluland (the land of flat cliffs), Markland (the land of forests), and Vinland (the land of vines). On the last he stayed through the winter, and came home in the spring.

Leif's brother Torvald also wanted to see the new land, and went off on a voyage of exploration. It was he who met the natives, the *Skrälings*, and got into a fight with them. He himself was killed. Another brother, Torsten, set out to bring home Torvald's body, but he never got there, and it was only Torfinn Karlsevne, with a whole band of Norsemen, who was first able to found a colony in America, in spite of resistance from the natives.

This settlement may well have been abandoned, but it was occupied afresh, and it was known in Greenland that one could obtain drift-wood there, beautiful pelts and walrus tusks. The voyage from Green-land was not long— shorter than that from Jutland to England—and although connections with the settlement were sometimes bad, it was natural for a bishop of 'Greenland and the neighbouring regions' immediately after the Viking era to stay there 'a long time, in both summer and winter.' It is also worth noting that the Icelandic bishop of Greenland sent the bishopric in Bergen furs from animals of species that were not known in Iceland or Greenland, but which were common on the American continent. We must assume, there-fore, that there was sustained contact with America, more regular than is suggested by the scattered saga texts.

The Norsemen's route along the east coast of America evidently went past Baffin Island and Hudson Bay, which did not invite a visit,

The Vikings penetrated right down to the wooded regions of north-east America, where they came upon Indians. It was here that they made acquaintance with the Indians' arrows. We can assume that mee-

tings generally went off peacefully, but it only needed a suspicious attitude to make the two peoples reach for their weapons.

Kavdlunak was the Eskimos' name for the Norsemen. The wooden figure, left, which was carved by Eskimos in the 14th or 15th centuries, shows a descendant of the Vikings in Greenland. It was found at Kitsorsaq in the Upernavik district. Right, a Cape Dorset Eskimo, carved from walrus ivory some time in the 11th century. Ca. 6 cms. high. Found at Inuarfigssuaq in the Thule district. Both figures are in the National Museum, Copenhagen.

A flint arrow-head which is undoubtedly Indian has been found in the Norse churchyard at Sandnes, Greenland (see map, p. 122). It comes from north-east America, and is one of the manifest proofs of the Norsemen's journeys to the west. The arrow is shown here in reconstruction. National Museum, Copenhagen.

on to Labrador, where the country is covered by forests, and so to Newfoundland, level with the Strait of Belle Isle. Here, it seems, on the island's north coast, was Vinland. This tallies well with the very detailed information we have from Icelandic sources and the maps of America, which were drawn on the basis of Nordic sources. Here the remains of Nordic-type houses have recently been found which could be appropriate for a colony, with dwelling-houses, cattle-byres and smithies. Here, moreover, it is easy to land on the shelving beach, and here the only inhabitants were Indians and Eskimos. The latter reached right down to these parts.

That there was contact and fighting between the Norsemen and the natives we know from a number of accounts. Some are completely incredible, but one discovery provides conclusive proof and contradicts all talk of fantasy. This is an Indian arrowhead found at Sandnes in Greenland, in one of the Norse cemeteries. It had been brought there by Norsemen, embedded perhaps in someone who had been killed, like Torvald. His brother Torsten, a farmer at Sandnes, declared before he died: 'It is a bad practice, which has taken hold here in Greenland since Christianity was introduced, to bury people

in unconsecrated ground and only make a little show of singing over them.' The latter might well be remedied; the former sometimes required dangerous journeys like Torsten's.

Dire events overtook the distant colonies. A new immigration of Eskimos reached them a good century after the Viking settlement of south Greenland. Although Norseman and *Skräling* managed to settle their disputes, relations between them could be tense. Connections with Iceland and Scandinavia came to an end. America was abandoned, then Västerbygden, and finally Österbygden. When a ship came to the coast of Greenland in about 1540, the skipper, Jon, and his men found on a little island dwellings, fish-sheds, and a number of drying-houses for fish. A dead man lay face downwards in the dust. On his head he had a well-sewn hood; the rest of his clothes were of a coarse woollen material and sealskin. By his side lay a curved sheath-knife, the blade almost completely worn by constant sharpening. They took the knife with them as a souvenir of the visit.

Such was the tale of Jon Greenlander. It paints a picture of the last of a hard-pressed line, who took the blows of fate as his forefathers had, defying the challenge of nature. They were not many, but their strength of will has a greatness like the character of Greenland. One thinks of them when one sees the coast looming massively over the blue-green sea, softened by the green of summer and richly coloured plants, and crowned with glaciers.

Einarsfjord, where Einar was the first to settle, in Österbygden, Greenland.

Roughly carved wooden head of a man from Northman's Farm in Univiarssuk, Västerbygden, Greenland.

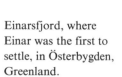

81

Dukes of Normandy
and Southern Italy

South-west of Denmark stretches the North Sea coast, flat and marshy. Rivers come from across the continent, convenient arteries for traffic, and run out through wide beds. Only further south, with the English Channel, does the landscape rise higher. Great peninsulas jut out like mighty breakwaters, with natural harbours for seafarers. Here and there is vegetation—abundant grass, bushes and trees. There is plenty of rain, and the soil is fertile. Altogether a landscape

One of the most instructive scenes shown in the Bayeux tapestry is the landing on the coast of England.

A level strip of beach was chosen on purpose for the landing; horses were brought over from France and there was no counting on using the harbour. So the ships lay to as near as they could get and the horses were led over the gunwales and waded out through the shallow water in order to get to dry land.

A band of Vikings, slashing-swords full of menace in front of them and shields by their side as protection. The helmets made them look even more warlike. Detail from the Gotland picture-stone from Smiss in Stenkyrka.

to rouse the cupidity of the Norsemen. They set to with all their energy to gain influence and secure their position in this well-situated region, which in time they colonized, and which takes its name from them: Normandy.

Further north they stopped at several places to sink in their teeth. In the wide Rhine delta, where the Frisians carried on a lively business in crafts and trades, lay the important town of Dorestad. An area

It is hard to imagine that these nobly decorated spear-tips were fitted on to casting-spears, which might easily be lost in the heat of battle. They could undoubtedly have been used more deliberately and surely as thrusting weapons. Ca. 20—25 cms. long. State Historical Museum, Stockholm.

like this was bound to attract the Vikings, who saw a profit in seeking out trading-centres, but who also took more downright booty. Dorestad itself was plundered and burnt. In 834 a Danish fleet ran in and took a rich booty without difficulty. Development in this flourishing town was cut short; the Vikings had all too much scope. For a time, Frisians who had fled still followed its fate with sympathy. A rich widow who lived in Birka donated money to the poor in her home-town. But gradually it became fatal to stay there, and the inhabitants left.

We know that there were North Sea towns where Wilhelmshaven and Emden now lie. The sites were the same. Around the year 800 wooden houses stood on either side of a long street. Here there was no room for peasants, only for trade and handicrafts. In towns such as these the Vikings supported themselves in tranquil conditions, though roughnecks with no idea of a peaceful, regular income took what they wanted without mercy.

As early as 808 the Danish ruler Godfred took up arms. Einhard, Charlemagne's biographer, writes with a mixture of shuddering and irony: 'He regarded Friesland and Saxony entirely as his own possessions and will shortly be coming to Aachen with a large force of troops.' It must have been a relief when the report was spread that Godfred had been murdered by one of his own men. Later came the Norsemen, mostly to pillage, not really to conquer. They had a safe target. North-west France was the scene of conflicting interests. The landed proprietors were playing an ever greater part. They fought amongst each other just like the rulers of the kingdoms, and kept a constant watch on one other, for fear that someone would become too powerful. Thus in times of weak or contending rulers, a situation was created which the Vikings exploited in masterly fashion. They offered their services, and sometimes went over to the side that promised more. During the year 862 alone, Charles the Bald hired

The houses and fortifications in towns of the Viking era were for the most part built of wood, and it only needed a few daring attackers to get the flames to spread. This is an imaginary view of one of Dorestad's fatal catastrophes.

the Viking chieftain Weland and his army for 5,000 pounds of silver, to drive away other Vikings from an island in the Seine; while Robert d'Anjou engaged a Viking force for 6,000 pounds of silver to fight a duke in Brittany. This reached its culmination when the Viking chieftain Rollo received Normandy as a duchy in 911. Charles the Simple made a move here which might have seemed fatal, but which in fact proved to be of advantage to the Frankish Empire. Previously, it had been necessary to pour out money to the Norsemen, who operated here, there and everywhere. One could feel safe only for a time. Now Rollo and his army took over responsibility for the important coast. When they had acquired the right to live there, these Vikings defended their new country. They felt at home, spread out over the countryside—as the many Nordic place-names testify—and came to dominate politically at the same time as they adapted themselves to the customs of the population. Their idea of justice and their trading, however, became important additions to social life, as was the increase in the number of free farms. Christianity was only one of the many original features that survived in the new community.

The Nordic language permeated the country. We see from many names that some people came to Normandy via England, and not

When Viking ships from the open sea entered the river-mouths, the sail was reefed and the crew had to take to the oars.

This sword was found in Dybeck, Skåne. The hilt is made of gilded silver. The ornamentation is south-English in origin, but the hilt was probably carried out by a Scandinavian artist-craftsman. State Historical Museum, Stockholm.

only direct from Scandinavia. This makes one think of the fortune-hunting bands that made their way to the Seine from England in 896 (see p. 25). Their efforts to win riches were successful indeed. But we should not on that account suppose that they headed home from France with their booty. They asked for permission to hold markets in the towns, and then had the chance to barter what they had taken through plunder or trade for goods which the local population offered of their own free will. This extensive barter-trade followed in the wake of the warlike expeditions and must have im-

Glass beaker from the Rhine district, found in one of the graves at Birka, on Björkö. From Birka alone more than 150 beakers, mirrors and other articles of glass, made in the Frankish Empire, have been collected. When the beautiful so-called funnel-beaker lacked a base, it had to be drained before it could be set down. State Historical Museum, Stockholm.

How one drank from a funnel-beaker appears from a contemporary illustration in the Wandalbert martyrology for the month of November. The Vatican Museum, Rome.

plied a boom in town life. Here was a great offering of wares, and it must be assumed that anyone who had been plundered could buy back his belongings on favourable terms. It is not surprising that the Emperor forbade his subjects to sell weapons to the Vikings. All the same, many weapons must have come into the hands of these bands—partly through plunder—and made their way north. Many fine French blades have been found there in the graves of warriors.

The confused conditions thus became stimulating for trade in a way that could not have been foreseen. There was a brisk turnover in objects of value and consumer goods, which till then had been in the firm hands of estates and monasteries, churches and towns. Now their perpetual owners were changed through the journeys of the Vikings. The large sums of money paid out to the Norsemen came back into circulation when they bought provisions, horses, weapons, clothes, farms, etc. It is typical that after the capitulation of Angers in 873, the Vikings reserved the right to stay some time in the town

Triangular silver ornament with the remains of gilding. That it is Frankish work appears from the characteristic acanthus motif. Brooches such as this were originally used to hold together three straps or three edges of material, and they are also known from the north, where the plant motif was then often imitated. This foreign ornament, which was found at Huseby, South Tröndelag, Norway, was probably used as a pendant, since there is a hole bored through at the top. Trondheim Museum.

and 'open a market.' They obviously had a clear idea that this form of contact with the inhabitants was no less lucrative than the plundering expeditions, which they undertook for the sake of variety.

It is related that Rollo's son, William Longsword, had to send his son from the capital Rouen to Bayeux, where Danish was spoken more than French, in order to learn the language. The Norse language spread with the conquerors over the whole of Normandy, but gradually gave way to French, which then became, in its old form, the tongue of the inhabitants. Nevertheless, the many Nordic place-names, especially at the mouth of the Seine, show that to begin with Danish was used by the immigrants and became accepted. That place-names in particular penetrated along the great river, is characteristic. This was where the leading merchants passed, and this was where it was especially favourable to settle. Typical suffixes such as *gard, torp* and *tot (toft)* may even be combined with Nordic proper names, which may also prefix place-names in *-ville*. Osmundiville derives from *Asmundr* and *-ville,* and Yvetot from *Ivetoft,* to name only a couple of examples.

Characteristic adornments and weapons have been preserved which may originate from heathen graves, including amongst other things oval women's brooches, which are always a distinctive feature of Nordic women's dress. It is probable that the chieftains here in Normandy, as well as further south on the Île de Croix, were buried in their ships with all their gaudy equipment of weapons, domestic and foreign. But before long, those who were not Christians gave up heathen burial-practices and followed the faith and customs of the country. They accepted French habits and had their hair cut short at the neck.

In its way, the social system in Normandy, a pronounced feudal dominion, suited the Norsemen in their relations with the native population, as they could govern more easily. They themselves manifestly considered each other equal, as we hear time and again. Nevertheless, the Norsemen gradually merged into this squirearchical environment. They were few in comparison with the large local population, and in order to rule they had to make use of whatever means were at hand, otherwise they could not have maintained their position. They formed contacts with influential families and married into them.

To begin with there were only a few free farmers. The majority of rural workers stood in economic and direct dependence on the landed proprietors, for whom they had to work a certain number of days. In return they had the right to protection in times of war.

The great land-owners promised as vassals to be loyal to the king, but this did not prevent some of them from seeking power themselves. It needed a strong personality, like Charlemagne, to make himself felt and curb the inner dissensions. Charlemagne already perceived that the economy could be improved by rational methods, and he issued an edict for the royal demesnes which shows us in an interesting way what life was like on the manor. Clearly, this was something that made an impression on the Norsemen.

A royal demesne was a comprehensive establishment among broad acres (with crop rotation), woods and meadows. Besides dwellings and farm-buildings, there had to be room for craftsmen such as smiths, carpenters, potters, soap-boilers, bakers, rope-makers, net-makers (for hunting and fishing equipment), brewers, etc. The

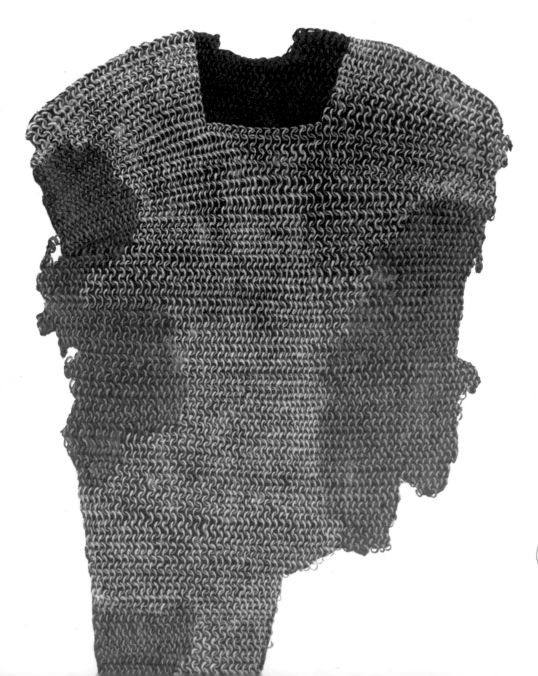

The ships being loaded before the voyage: a scene from the Bayeux tapestry. Weapons and mail-shirts are carried on board hung in practical fashion on a long pole, which three men are able to carry, while a strong Viking has taken a barrel on one shoulder—it may be supposed that it contained strong liquor.

Chain-mail found in the burial-mound at Jarlshaug, Tröndelag, Norway. Each ring was riveted with two rivets, and they were joined to each other as shown in the sketch. It was a time-consuming and laborious task, and mail was expensive to buy, which was why only chieftains and the eminent could afford it. University Collection of Antiquities, Oslo.

dwelling-house itself was on a noble scale, with, amongst other things, beds, pillows, quilts, table-cloths, carpets, and vessels of wood, iron and copper. The women had enough to do, although they had help from the craftsmen; they prepared flax and wool, dyed material, and saw to the preserving of foodstuffs, such as meat, bacon, sausage, honey, mead and mustard. The estate had to send, amongst other things, two-thirds of the solid produce to the king, and always had to have two fatted oxen for his sustenance when he came on a visit. Excess produce had to be sold, and a kind of market arose in the courtyard.

Domestic animals were kept in large numbers, oxen, horses—which were also used in cultivation as working animals—pigs, sheep and goats. Chicken and geese received waste from the mill, and supported themselves for the most part in its vicinity. As tokens of the manor's noble standing there would be pheasants, peacocks (whose brilliant plumage so impressed the Norsemen that they took some home with them. The gaily-coloured Olav På [Peacock] is named after them), ducks, doves, partridge and bees. In the orchards several types of apples, pears, cherries, etc., and of flowers and herbs there were as many as seventy-two varieties, from roses and lilies to chervil and onions.

The master himself could be entertained by hunting, riding and swimming. There was bathing not only in lakes, rivers and the sea, but also in hot springs.

Frankish dress we know through Einhard's description of Charlemagne: 'Next to his body he wore his linen shirt and short linen trousers; over this he had a tunic with a silk border; socks and shoes on his feet and cloth bands round his legs. In winter he protected his shoulders and chest with a fur jerkin and threw a cloak about him. He was always girt with a sword, which had a hilt and scabbard of gold or silver; at times, on special occasions or when he received foreign envoys, he wore a sword studded with precious stones.'

The ruler's immediate assistants we know from contemporary sources. The arch-chaplain looked after ecclesiastical matters, and was his private priest. The chancellor attended to correspondence, etc. The count palatine had to deal in particular with laws and judgments, while financial matters—which included the royal demesnes—came under the treasurer. Amongst other officials one might name the chamberlain, the cup-bearer and the master of the royal stables, some crown foresters and the falconers. Altogether a comprehensive body.

The conclusive political decisions were made twice a year in the presence of the vassals. These meetings might well give rise to embarrassments, such as the attitude of the church, which was determined just as much by political as by spiritual motives.

In this society, which placed quite new demands on the Norsemen, the foreigners grew up and made themselves felt, first and foremost, of course, as warriors. A vivid picture of this seigniorial life, but also of that of the ordinary peasant, is given in the Bayeux tapestry. It shows that the habits of the Vikings still survived as late as the 11th century. The Bayeux tapestry is an embroidered roll of linen no less than seventy metres long and half a metre wide. Despite its great age it is very impressive, with fine colours. The pictures are composed in a masterly manner and are full of life. One can relive the Vikings' journeys in foreign lands and get numerous authentic details. It is like a roll of film; the artist gives a rich account of events, with discreet prominence to Bishop Odo, evidently his employer. He has a sense of humour, moreover, and a feeling for drastic little incidents. As far as one can judge, the work was carried out in southern England and was intended for the new cathedral in Bayeux.

The main frieze covers the wide middle part. Above and below run narrow bands of pictures with decorations and little scenes of everyday life. In particularly dramatic situations the main scene encroaches on the narrow parts, which then accompany the action. The invasion of England itself is a fascinating documentary account, so much the more significant since it gives us, in passing, details which we would not know from any other source. Ordinary occurrences are mentioned all too rarely in the historical sources from this period.

When Duke William, on Odo's urgent advice, decides to take possession of England, his (putative) inheritance, he first has a large number of ships built. Trees are felled and split, with the broad-bladed axe. Beams are squared and ship's carpenters go to work effectively with drill and axe. Ship after ship lies ready on the beach, as yet without sails or dragon-heads. The moment the signal for invasion is given, long ropes are slung round thick wooden posts out in the water and the ships are hauled out, filled with men, horses and weapons—swords, bows, spears, chain-mail and pointed helmets. Provisions and barrels of wine are already on board. The wind fills the sails. In his ship with the banner bearing a cross at the mast-head and his standard at the stern, William leads the crossing. They land at Pevensey, on a flat beach. The horses they lead with them, over the gunwales. The masts are lowered and the dragon-heads removed. One does not want to upset the spirits of the land.

The invasion over-runs—as always—the local population. Riders make their way to farms, slaughter cows, sheep and lambs, steal bread and even burn down houses. The women and children look on with sorrow. Meanwhile, the English soldiers fortify themselves in castles and towns, but William's troops dig up to the walls and set fire to the wooden defence-works.

Not until now do the scouts make contact with the English army under King Harold, and after the signal for battle, the cavalry spur on their horses and charge across the battlefield. The tension mounts and events fly across this splendidly depicted scene, in which a detachment of eager bowmen highlight the riders' speed as they slash into the tight formation of Anglo-Saxon infantry. These seem to flinch slightly, but hold their ground, and throwing-weapons fly on all sides. Now macabre details crop up in the borders, hacked-off limbs and heads, corpses on the battlefield, and finally the plundering of those who have fallen. At the same time, the main scene shows details in clear pictures: sword-blows, rearing horses, the long-handled battle-axe, which makes great slanting cuts, arrows piercing shields

The battle is played out with violence and realism in the rendering by the Bayeux master. Spears are thrust into opponents. Axes slash at horses' heads and men fall to sword-blows so hefty that they are even capable of severing an axe-blade from its shaft. The standard-bearer, round whom men rallied, has dropped his

standard and fallen from his horse. Cavalry battles took place at speed and the clash of steel made horse and rider fly through the air. It is obvious that the artist of the Bayeux tapestry had seen and experienced a battle such as this in reality, so vividly does he reproduce the episodes.

side by side, men in agile movement. Harold gets an arrow in the eye and then falls from a blow by a rider's sword. One is present in the whole clamour of the battle, experiencing all the macabre episodes familiar to a Viking. It is hard, unvarnished reality.

The Normans were not content with the conquest of England. They had other fields of activity for their energy. The Arabs had pressed through North Africa up into Spain, and for the time being left southern Italy in peace. They ruled from Córdoba, with its fine houses, palace and 600 mosques, a great city. Here, civilization flourished, and it is said that in the middle of the 10th century the Caliph had 400,000 volumes in his library.

There was thus wealth to be had here by plunder and trade, and the Vikings soon found their way to the Spanish coasts, where through booty they acquired no little of it. The Moors, however, were ready to fight, and in addition were interested in trade connections. They sent envoys to the Viking ruler in order to establish contact. But for long after they remembered the red sails that filled the sea off Lisbon, and 'struck fear and terror into the hearts of men'.

In southern Italy the last of the Viking conquests were carried out in just the same way as the first. Around the year 1000, the south Italian princes were at war with one another. The ruler of Salerno sought help from forty Norman pilgrims and recruited more when

Here the battle-scenes continue from the previous sample. The Bayeux tapestry, 70.34 m. long and 0.5 m. high, relates how Duke William of Normandy and his men—descendants of the Vikings—invaded England in 1066. The tapestry has been kept, ever since it was made in the 11th century, at Bayeux in Normandy. It is embroidered with woollen yarn on linen material.

they were on their way home. In this way a body of Norman mercenaries was formed, who acquired land and gladly offered their services to one prince after the other, until they themselves had outmanoeuvred the original holders of power. A prominent family of rulers, sons of Tancred de Hauteville, managed the politics with suppleness, and to satisfy the ambitious warriors, southern Italy was divided into counties, but held together nevertheless by the strongest, who received the title of Duke. With this late but characteristic procedure the Viking age in the south drew to its close. The Normans had already merged into Christian civilisation and founded a series of dynasties which adapted themselves to the foreign environment.

On the River-Routes to the South-East

During the year 921—922 a caravan made its way from Bukhara over deserts, mountains and steppes to Bulgar on the middle reaches of the Volga, where the wide river turns off toward the north-west. Here lived the ruler of the bold and warlike Bulgars, whom the caravan was to visit. It was an Arabian embassy that had to evade their common enemy, the Khazars, on the southern reaches of the Don and the Volga. The Khazars were a constant source of irritation to both the Bulgars and the Arabs. They controlled the trade-routes from northern Russia to the Arab world, and did so without regard for others. Their opponents were thus forced into each others arms. The khan in Bulgar approached the Arabs for a meeting in order to go over to Islam, and he received them with great goodwill in his yurt a little way from the permanent sites. The throne was covered with Byzantine brocade, and his clothes followed the latest fashion in Baghdad, made by an expert from that city.

Ibn Fadlan, who accompanied the embassy, used his leisure hours to look about him. Down by the river there was a group of wooden houses which the Rus had built. Their ships lay moored immediately below. They had come to the market and offered slaves and furs against silver coins. The demand was lively. It was noticed that as far away as Ibn Fadlan's homeland there was interest in their wares. Their true outlet lay there, in the rich cities of the Orient, where agriculture depended on slaves for man-power. There the nobles were delighted with the sables and other beautiful furs obtained by the Rus hunters and other northern tribes. Nothing prevented the Rus from travelling further by boat to the mouth of the Volga among the Khazars, but it was a long journey via the export-harbour Itil and the Caspian Sea. So use was made of the market in Bulgar, where large amounts changed hands, to the delight not least of the khan, who collected 10 % of the turnover.

The Dnieper rapids. As we know from the Byzantine Emperor Constantine Porphyrogenitus, these rapids had both Nordic and Slavonic names. For example, the Nordic Ulvorsi, which in Slavonic was called Ostrovuniprach. Here the Vikings were forced to drag their boats along the banks in order to proceed.

With pride Ibn Fadlan would be able to display his acquisitions in Baghdad when at long last he got home again. The city was a swarming world compared with far-off Bulgar. Within the circular city-walls with their four gates ran a system of streets full of noisy and toiling people. The sun shone down burning hot on this conglomeration of bazaars, mosques, minarets, houses and palaces, large and small. From every quarter came goods for sale. And here, too, there was scope for the imagination. Story-tellers collected their hearers in the shade of the palm trees.

In the cool of the palace garden Ibn Fadlan told of his experiences on the journey. They sounded like fairy-tales, but were the sharp observations of a man of the world, the interpretations of a true believer. He fascinated his listeners just as much as the story-tellers outside, and his meeting with the Rus was his *tour de force*, an exotically primitive milieu with elements of fantasy.

'Never have I seen people with more perfect physique than these. They are as tall as date-palms and rubicund. They have on no tunic, nor caftan either, but the man wears a cloak which covers half of his body, so that he has one hand free.

'Each of them has an axe, a sword, a knife, which he never parts

Silver clasp from Voronezh, Russia. This beautiful woman's adornment is one of the most interesting testimonies of the Norsemen's journeys in Russia. It has a typically Scandinavian shape. Most of the ornamentations with animal-heads can be recognized from Swedish counterparts, but the interlaced patterns recall Russian (or Byzantine) models. It is probable, therefore, that the work was carried out by a Scandinavian in Russia or by a Slav artist-craftsman to the order of a Scandinavian woman. One arm of the silver clasp is missing, but we have reconstructed it here in its entirety. The Hermitage, Leningrad.

Belt-mounting, refashioned as a pendant. It was found at Vårby, Södermanland, Sweden, together with other objects from the east from the middle of the 10th century. The ornamentation is known from the Ukraine-Hungary and this was no doubt brought from there. Ca. 4 cms. high. State Historical Museum, Stockholm.

with. Their swords are broad and flat, grooved and of Frankish type.

'Their women all have a container fastened on their breast. It is of iron, silver, copper or gold, according to the size and worth of the husband's fortune. On each container there is a ring with a knife in it, which is also fastened to her breast. Round their necks they have neck-rings of gold and silver; for when a man is the owner of ten thousand dirhems he has a neck-ring made for his wife. The ornaments they appreciate most are the green glass beads that are found on ships. They go a long way to get hold of them, pay up to one dirhem for a bead, and thread them into a necklace for their women.

'They are the dirtiest of God's creatures. They do not clean themselves after excretion, nor after they have passed water, and they do not wash themselves after the ejaculation of sperm. Nor do they wash their hands after meals. Yes, they are like asses that have gone astray. They come from their homeland and lie to with their ships on the Itil (Volga) which is a great river, and build large wooden houses on its banks. In one of the houses ten or twenty of them, more or less, gather together. Each of them has a bench on which he sits, and with him sit the beautiful girls (slaves), which are at the merchant's disposal. And he makes love to his girl while his comrades look on.

'As soon as their ship arrives at this anchorage, they go ashore, and each has with him bread, meat, onions, milk and *nabid* (presumably ale or mead), and they go over to a tall, upright wooden post with a face that looks like a man's. Round about it are small figures, and behind these figures high wooden poles planted in the ground. He says: "Oh, my Lord, I have come from afar with so many girls and so many sable-skins"—and he counts up all the goods he has brought with him. "I come to you now with this offering." Then he lays what he has with him before the wooden post. "I pray that you get me a buyer who has many dinars and dirhems, and who pays what I want and does not contradict what I say." So he goes his way. And if business is bad and time goes on he returns with one or two more offerings. Often trade goes easily for him, so that he gets a sale. Then he goes over to a herd of goats or cattle and slaughters them. A part of the meat he gives away as alms. The rest he takes to the offering-place and throws it between the big post and the smaller ones surrounding it. The heads of the goats and cattle he hangs on the poles planted in the ground. And when night falls the dogs come and eat it all up. The one who has done this then says: "See, my Lord is pleased with me and has eaten my offerings."

'I was constantly hearing that when they buried their dead chieftains, they undertook things, the mildest of which was cremation. I was therefore very interested to find out about this. So one day I got to know that a man who was esteemed among them had died.

They laid him in a grave and covered it over, and there he had to lie for ten days until they had finished sewing and cutting his clothes. After that the following took place: for a poor man they prepared a small ship, laid him in it and burnt it; if it was a rich man, they gathered together all his wealth and divided it into three parts: a third goes to his family, a third goes on clothes for him, and a third for brewing *nabid,* which they drank on the day his slave-girl let herself be killed and burnt with her master. When one of their chieftains dies, his family say to his thralls and slave-girls: "Which of you will die with him?" Then one of them says: "I will." And the one who has said this is forced to stand by his word, and cannot withdraw. Most of those who do this are slave-girls.

'When the man whom I have already mentioned had died, they said to his slave-girls: "Who will die with him?" One of them replied: "I will." They then gave two slave-girls the task of seeing to her and being with her wherever she went; they even washed her feet with their own hands.

'When the day came for him and his slave-girl to be burnt, I went down to the river where his ship lay. It had now been pulled up on to dry land, and four props of birch and other wood had been

A gathering for a funeral by the bank of a river. Ships are drawn up. Men have come from the north, and are just witnessing the melancholy spectacle of cremation.

prepared. Around these had been built what looked like a great stack of wood. Then the ship was dragged over and placed on the pile of wood. Next came an old crone whom they called the Angel of Death, and spread rugs on the bench. She was responsible for the making of the clothes (for the dead man) and for the preparation (of the body). She is also the one who kills the girls. I saw that she was a large old woman, squat and gloomy-looking. Then they came over to his grave; they removed the earth from the woodwork and even removed the woodwork. After that they took off the clothes in which he had died. I noticed that he had become black on account of the cold in the land. With his burial-ale they had placed fruit and a lute. All this they took out. Strangely enough, the corpse did not stink, and had not changed in any way yet except for the colour of the skin. Then they dressed him in trousers, over-trousers, tunic and cloak of *dibag* with gold buttons, put a hood of silk brocade and sable on his head and carried him into the tent which stood on the ship, where they set him down on the rugs and propped him up with cushions. Then they came with *nabid,* fruit and sweet-smelling plants and laid them beside him. Then they came with a dog, cut it in two halves and threw them into the ship. Next, they came with all his weapons and

laid them by his side. Then they took two horses and let them gallop until they were sweaty. Whereupon they hacked them to pieces with swords and threw the meat into the ship. Similarly, they came with two cows, which they also hacked to pieces and threw into the ship. Then they came with a cock and a hen, killed them and threw them in. Meanwhile, the slave-girl who wished to be killed walked up and down. She went into one tent after the other, and the master of the tent made love to her, saying: "Tell your master: I have done this for love of you."

'When Friday afternoon came, they led the slave-girl over to something they had made which resembled a door-frame. Then she seated herself on the palms of the men's hands, and came so high that she stuck out over this door-frame, and said something in the language she spoke. After that they lowered her, but lifted her up again, and she did as she had done the first time. After that they lowered her and lifted her up for the third time, and she did as she had done the first two times. Next, they handed her a hen, and she cut off its head and threw it away. They took the hen and threw it into the ship. Then I asked the interpreter what it was that she did. He replied: "The first time they lifted her up, she said: 'Look! I see my father and mother.' The second time she said: 'Look! I see all my dead kinsmen sitting there.' The third time she said: 'Look! I see my master sitting in Paradise, and Paradise is fair and green, and with him are men and young lads (servants). He is calling me. Let me go to him.'"

'After that they led her away to the ship. She then took off two arm-bands she was wearing, and gave them to the old woman called the Angel of Death, who was the one who was to kill her. Then she took off two rings which she had round her ankles, and gave them to the daughters of the woman who was known as the Angel of Death. After that they led her up on to the ship, but did not let her go into the tent. Then some men came and had with them shields and wood (sticks) and handed her a cup of *nabid*. She sang over it and drank from it. The interpreter then said to me: "She is now taking leave of her girl-friends with this." After that she was handed another cup. She took it and made her singing long drawn out; but the old woman hurried her to get her to drink up and go into the tent, where her master was. Then I watched her, and she looked completely confused. She wanted to go into the tent but stuck in her head between it and the ship. Then the woman took her by the head and got it into the tent, and the woman herself went in with her. The men began to bang their shields so that the sound of her screams should not be heard, in case the other girls should be frightened and not want to seek death with their masters. Then six men went into the tent, and all of them made love to the girl. After that they laid her by the side

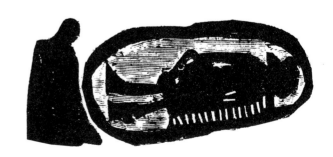

A scene full of mystery on the picture-stone from Lärbro, Stora Hammar, Gotland. The warrior who hangs in the swinging tree, the feathered shape and the group round the strange mound prompt many different interpretations. The picture may be of a sacrificial scene.

This remarkable representation on the Gotland picture-stone from Alskog presumably shows a dead person in his grave.

of her dead master. Two of them took her legs, two her hands. And the woman who was called the Angel of Death laid a rope (in a loop) round her neck (with the ends) in either direction, and passed them to two men, so that they should pull on them. Then she stepped forward with a little dagger with a broad blade and began to stick it in and out between the girl's ribs, while the two men throttled her with the rope, so that she died.

'After that, the one amongst the people who was most nearly related to the dead man came forward. He took a piece of wood and set fire to it. Then he walked backwards, with his back to the ship and his face (towards the people) and held the piece of wood in one hand, while the other lay against his back, and he was naked. In this way the wood which had been put under the ship was set on fire, after they had placed the slave-girl they had killed beside her master. Then the people came forward with wood and timber, and each one had with him a piece of wood with the end on fire. They threw this on to the wood (which lay under the ship) so that it set fire to the wood, then to the ship, then to the tent and the man and the slave-girl and all that was there. After that a strong and uncanny wind blew up, so that the flames grew more powerful and the fire blazed up even more.

'By my side stood a Rus, and I heard him talking to the interpreter who was with him. I asked him what he had said to him. He replied: "He said you Arabs are stupid." I asked: "Why so?" He replied: "Well, the person you love and honour most of all you lay in the earth, and the earth and vermin and worms devour him. We, on the other hand, burn him up in a second, so that he goes to Paradise that hour." And then he burst out in a loud laugh. When I asked him about this, he replied: "His (the dead man's) Lord has sent the wind to him in love, so that it will bear him away in an hour." And in fact an hour had not gone by, before the ship and the wood and the slave-girl and her master had become ashes and dust. After that, on the spot where the ship had stood when they dragged it up from the river, they built something that looked like a round hillock. In the middle of it they set up a great post of birchwood. On it they wrote the name of the man and the name of the Rus king, and then they went their way.'

After this gruesome description Ibn Fadlan passes over to a calmer tone—but his account still makes its points:

'It is the custom of the King over the Rus to have with him in the castle four hundred men of the heroes in his suite and of trustworthy men. They die with him, and let themselves be killed for him. Each of them has a slave-girl who looks after him, washes his head and puts before him whatever he will eat and drink, and another slave-girl with whom he sleeps. With him on the throne sit forty slave-girls who are intended for his bed.'

Let us leave this scene and move westwards along the river-routes, through the flat country side, to meet other Rus people, who are described by Arab travellers. Ibn Rustah, the astronomer and geographer, tells of a visit to an island in a lake: 'They had no land, but imported food-stuffs by boat and travelled about hunting for slaves. They traded with these captives in the same way as they did with valuable skins of sable, etc., in Hazaran and Bulgar on the Volga. The money they received they kept in their belts. They keep their clothes clean, and the men adorn themselves with arm-bands of gold. They treat their slaves well and wear exquisite clothes, since they do business with great industry. They have many towns. They are rough-handed towards each other, honour their guests and treat well strangers who seek refuge amongst them and all who visit them. If some of them are challenged to fight, they all turn out. They do not split up but stand as one man against their enemies, until they have conquered them. If one of them has a complaint to bring against

The steelyard is of the same type as that still in use today. It is a clear example of a practical shape and provides evidence of the Vikings' interest in trade. The steelyard was of great importance in all bargaining as payment was often made by weight of silver. Find from Mästermyr, Gotland. Length, 35.3 cms. State Historical Museum, Stockholm.

Silver amulet furnished with an inscription in Arabic on each side. 6.9 cms. in diameter. It was found in Uppland, Sweden, and is now in the State Historical Museum, Stockholm.

another, he takes him up before the prince, where they both present their case. If he gives a decision in the dispute between them, then it becomes as he will. But if, in his judgment, they cannot come to an agreement, then he orders them to decide the matter themselves with the sword. So they both fight against each other. And the one who is superior then settles the dispute in the way he wishes.

'They are possessed of heroism and bravery, and when they come into another tribe's area they will not give up until they have crushed them completely. They take their women into captivity and make them (the men) into slaves. They are tall of body and are handsome and bold. But their boldness does not appear on land. Their attacks and expeditions are undertaken only by ship.

'They wear leg-wrappings. Each of these takes about 100 ells of material.

'When one of them has a son, the father goes over to the newly-born with a drawn sword. He then takes it and throws it in front of the boy-child and says: "I leave you no property as inheritance; you own nothing but what you can get for yourself with this your sword."

'When one of their great men dies, they make a grave like a large house, and place him in it. With him they lay his clothes and the gold arm-rings he wore, and also much food, jugs of liquor and coins.

A river in northern Russia. It is calm, the sails are down and the oars come into use.

The mighty warrior, well equipped and wearing baggy knee-breeches, is received by a woman who hands a filled drinking-horn up to the thirsty man. It may be a dead warrior being welcomed to Valhalla. Detail from a Gotland picture-stone from Lillbjärs in Stenkyrka.

The rune-stone which the Norseman Grani raised on the island of Berezany at the mouth of the Dnieper. The text reads: 'Grani made this stone grave after Karl, his comrade.' The stone is now in the museum at Odessa.

They also lay his favourite wife in the grave with him, while she is still alive. Then the door of the grave is closed and she dies there.'

The descriptions of the Rus consist of a strange mixture of Nordic and foreign elements. We shall return later to the authenticity of these accounts and regard the sources merely as testimony about how the Norsemen appeared outside their homeland, after having lived in a foreign country for a few generations. The accounts describe conditions at the beginning of the 10th century, but we have proof of Swedish activity in Russia as early as 839, when they are mentioned in the sources. Accompanying an embassy from the Byzantine Emperor Theophilos to the Frankish Emperor Louis were some envoys who had come to Theophilos from the ruler of the Rus. They could not return home direct, because the regions between had been invaded by hostile neighbours, so they made their way to their homeland by travelling through the Frankish Empire. As an explanation to his imperial colleague, Theophilos wrote that the envoys had said they were of Swedish nationality, and that they had been sent by the Khagan of the Rus (a title we recognize from the Turkish peoples in the east). It is obvious that this kingdom had been in contact with the eastern kingdoms on the middle and lower reaches of the Volga and at the mouth of the Don.

Earlier still, there had been settlers from Sweden and Gotland on the east coast of the Baltic. At Grobin in Latvia three grave-sites have been found next to each other. In two of them were burial-gifts, weapons and ornaments which otherwise are known only from Gotland. The third, with low grave-mounds, contained objects which were typical for the Mälar district. The burials ceased towards the year 800. Right next to them is a large fortification with finds that correspond to those from upper Sweden. This indicates that people from the Mälar area, whose warrior-graves we know especially well, crossed the Baltic as conquerors, established themselves, and were joined by people from the rich trading island of Gotland. The Gotlanders saw the advantages of settling close to the fortress and received hardly less profit than the warriors.

It must have been people of this type who penetrated further east and seized power there in the years previous to 839. They maintained themselves in towns such as Staraya Ladoga on the river Volkhov, south of Ladoga, and Novgorod. At various places finds have been made of Nordic inscriptions in runes on wood, and at Staraya Ladoga, which is the oldest, Nordic ornaments and weapons have been dug up. Precisely in the areas south of Ladoga groups of burial-sites have been found with small mounds, which cover cremations, and ornaments such as the oval brooches of Scandinavian type. Here is clear evidence of migration. The network of rivers stretched so far that one could travel without great difficulty to remote parts in one's own

Connections with the Far East were present before the Viking era. The conditions that favoured the growth of Birka, a trading-town and rich resort for merchant-farmers, had existed for centuries. The island of Helgö in Lake Mälar is one of the most amazing examples of the start of this expansion. Here exotic *objets d'art* have been found, such as this Buddha figure from Central Asia, which show that there were contacts with the whole of the then-known world, from India to Ireland. 8.4 cms. high. State Historical Museum, Stockholm.

The Norsemen, on their journeys to the East, came upon remarkable things, camels, Moslems, and the indescribable riches of the caravans. Whether they themselves travelled with the caravans is doubtful. One or two, however, may well have chanced to follow the slowly swaying transports across deserts of sand and stone.

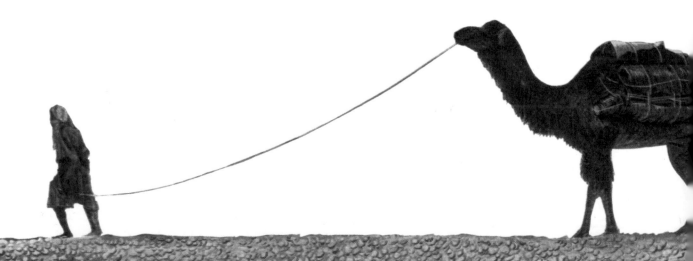

The Arabian silver coin, the dirhem, is a development of the Greek drachma, and its name a modification of the Greek. Thousands of these coins came to Scandinavia. During the 9th century the different types of coin correspond, with regard to place of manufacture and time, in Scandinavia and in the Russian finds. We can reckon, therefore, that the coins came from the Arabs via Russia. But around 900 there is a change in the composition of the coins in the finds, and in Scandinavia quantities of fresh coins appear from the Arab countries east of the Caspian Sea. Since there are only a few older coins among them, it is probable that there were direct links between the eastern kingdoms and Scandinavia. Presumably the silver coins were brought away from foreign countries by the Norsemen themselves.

In the illustration, the coin on the left is from the beginning of the 7th century and was found in Birka. It is stamped with a picture of Zoroaster's altar of fire between two guardians. The other two coins were found at Sorunda, Södermanland, Sweden.

boat. Sometimes the boat had to be carried across a tongue of land from one river to the next.

The route to the Volga went via Svir and Onega to the south across Lake Beloye. Through tracts of forest, one reached the river itself, which leads past Bulgar and down to the mouth at Itil. This large trading-place was dominated by the Khazars, who had been converted to the Jewish faith. They had their royal palace on an island in the middle of the river, both banks of which were built upon, and here lived Mohammedans, Christians, Jews and heathens. Among the latter were also people from the north.

From the middle reaches of the Volga, caravan routes led to Samarkand, Merv, Tashkent and other cities and regions in the east, where rich silver mines had been opened. This was ruled by an independent Mohammedan dynasty, the Tahirids, from 822 to 873. They, more than anyone else in the Arab world, could supply thousands of silver coins and in exchange obtained luxury goods. This stream of silver from the mines continued even when the Samanids took over power in the north-eastern Mohammedan kingdom. The coins were dispersed, amongst other ways, along the caravan route across the middle Volga to the north. In northern Afghanistan a deposit of silver of unprecedented richness was struck during the second half of the 8th century, but after that the mines gradually became poorer, so that in the course of the 10th century they completely lost their importance. In the years around 930 the eastern Arab countries experienced crises because of the lack of silver, which was a check to trade.

Another important trade route from the north followed the Dnieper to the Black Sea; right at the mouth of the river, on the island of Berezany, a rune-stone has been found raised by Grani in memory of his comrade Karl. The route led to Dnieper, west of what is now

Smolensk, in the vicinity of which a large burial-place has been found, which was used by the Vikings. Ornaments of characteristic Nordic forms have been met with here. The Dnieper flows past Kiev, which became the capital of one of the Rus kingdoms. Here too Nordic ornaments have been found. Further south the river passes through a series of rapids mentioned by the Byzantine Emperor Constantine Porphyrogenitus in his writings on how an empire should be ruled. He leaves a good deal of important information about Scandinavian activity and mentions double-names for these rapids. One group of names is Scandinavian, the other Slavic, e.g. *Eifur—Neasit (Eifur* means in Old Norse 'ever violent,' *Neasit* is in Old Slavic 'the insatiable'). Curiously enough, *Eifur* is mentioned on a Swedish runestone as the distant goal of two brothers.

A third route went direct from the Baltic harbours at the mouths of the Oder and Vistula towards the south-east to Dniester. It crossed the important trade route from the west through Cracow. The foremost connecting-route was the Oder, in the mouth of which lay the island of Wollin. Its town, Jumne, is mentioned by Adam of Bremen in extravagant terms, and fresh excavations have in fact established a typically Slavic town, surrounded by a strong wall, reinforced with wood. The houses lay close together in a fairly regular pattern, a well-planned and rich urban development.

Many Slavic towns lie scattered in these parts, like forts that protect a great man's farm. Towns often grew up near such a fortification. Not without reason the Scandinavians called this vast area *Gardarike,* the kingdom of towns. They travelled widely all around it.

Some of its first rulers, Rurik for example, have names which go straight back to Nordic forms (Rörekr). Such names disappear, however, during the 10th century; clearly, the Norsemen married into Slavic dynasties. The wide area was far too large to be held in check by a handful of Vikings, however energetic they were. Culturally they adapted themselves to the new conditions, which also appears from the design of weapons and ornaments: some are of purely Nordic type; others are very reminiscent of these but exhibit distinctive features. They were probably made in Viking colonies, and not only by Nordic craftsmen. When we connect the name Rus with the Nordic immigrants, therefore, this is only partly justified. The name may be Scandinavian (although its origin may be interpreted in different ways), but the people were hardly a uniform group of emigrants. They may have been a Swedish-Finnish-Slavic people, who had come from the north.

The Varangians, at any rate, were Scandinavian Vikings; they were merchants and warriors. They travelled further, to the Byzantine Empire. Beyond the long river-routes, fresh, rich opportunities opened out on the Black Sea and the Mediterranean. Here lay the shattered

On the island of Wollin in the mouth of the Oder lay a large, well-planned Slav town with fortifications. In later literary tradition, the Viking fortress of Jomsborg is linked with the place, but although the Norsemen may have dominated the town during a period of transition—King Harald Bluetooth died here—there is nothing to indicate that it ever had a permanent garrison of Vikings. Adam of Bremen (c. 1070) tells of 'the illustrious town of Jumne, which affords the barbarians and Greeks (i.e. Greek-Catholic merchants) who live around it a much-used anchorage;' and he goes on: 'It is without a shadow of doubt the greatest of all the cities of Europe, and it is inhabited by Slavs and other peoples, Greeks and barbarians; for even Saxons travelling to it have leave to live there on similar conditions, only if they do not reveal their Christianity for as long as they are there. For everyone there is still bound by heathen errors. But when it comes to character and hospitality, no people can be found who are more honest or friendly. The town is rich in wares from all the Nordic peoples, and all that is good and rare may be found there.'

Roman Empire, and here the Mohammedan rulers had forced their way in. The Eastern Emperor was particularly interested in attaching Varangians to him because they were independent, and did not feel bound to any of the many contending factions in the city, but only to the Emperor himself.

The Byzantine Empire was certainly worth a visit for travellers from the north or Russia. In the capital, Constantinople, the Emperor followed the political game attentively. It is presented to us by Constantine Porphyrogenitus in his work on how an empire should be ruled. He held sway over a hierarchy of courtiers and functionaries. Within the shelter of his walls, he ran a comprehensive administration, with the Varangians as a picturesque feature, a sort of Swiss Guard. Even the captains of the Guard were foreigners, like Ragnvald from Ed (north of Stockholm), who laconically states his rank:

> These runes
> Ragnvald had cut.
> He was in Greece.
> He was chief of a military unit.

Everywhere in Constantinople lived craftsmen and merchants, who were well organised in guilds. They were influential, and determined the opportunities for foreigners to buy and sell. Here were wealthy silk-weavers, soap-boilers, linen merchants, butchers and many others, who set their own prices. The foreigners were only allowed to buy a certain amount of luxury goods in exchange for the value they had brought with them, which was agreed, amongst other things, in the commercial treaty of 945 with the Grand Duke of the Rus. It is striking that in the earlier treaty of 912 the names of the envoys are predominantly Scandinavian and Finnish, whereas the later embassy consists chiefly of Slavic persons. Foreigners were allowed to buy silk for at most 50 gold coins, and they could only do business if they had a special authorisation issued by the Russian Grand Duke. In return they received free upkeep and maintenance in the imperial city. The influence of the Norsemen seems to have been on the way back during the 10th century.

These trading visits are mentioned in both Constantine's book and the oldest Rus annals. There we learn that a number of Slavic and other tribes were liable to taxation by the Russian Grand Duke, who sent a part of the large proceeds to Constantinople to obtain Byzantine goods in exchange.

On the connection between Constantinople and the Rus kingdom, we have an amusing account, seen from both sides, which vividly illustrates the cultural atmosphere. The Rus version is a saga-like tale, while the Byzantine one is a pure bit of reporting.

One of the main characters was the Emperor Constantine, the other Princess Olga of Slavic descent, married to the son of the Varangian Prince Rurik, Igor of Novgorod, well-known from a visit in 941. Then he had attacked Constantinople with a fleet. Now Olga wanted to pay the Emperor a peaceful visit, though not entirely without political and economic undercurrents. Constantine received

A marble lion, four metres high, with loops of runes carved by Nordic Varangians, stood in Piraeus, the port of Athens. The Venetians captured the town in 1687 and took the lion to Venice, where it still remains. It has not been possible to interpret the inscription.

Christianity spread early in the East. From the Byzantine Empire it extended to Russia and the Balkan countries. Below, three Christian pictures which reached Sweden around the 11th century. Uppermost, a fragment cut from an article of silver, probably a head of Christ, from the silver hoard from Valdarve, Eskelhelm, Gotland. 1.75 × 1.45 cms. in diameter. Beneath this, the two sides of a pill-box reliquary in silver from a hoard at Valbo, Gästrikland, Sweden. On one side the Madonna, and on the other St. Nicholas. 2 cms. in diameter. This is a Russian-Byzantine piece, now at the State Historical Museum, Stockholm.

There was a splendour and might about the city of Constantinople—or Miklagård, as the Norsemen called the great metropolis. Protected by its high walls, it rose above the Bosphorus. Here we look towards the Imperial palace itself, surrounded by the lofty cupolas of sumptuous churches, and the Hippodrome with its two obelisks on the left. The Palace was a magnificent labyrinth, created for Byzantine court-ceremonial, which cut visitors down to size by leading them across open courts, down long corridors and through glittering apartments, to leave them finally, overcome, before the golden seat of state in the throne-room.

her with full pomp and circumstance. Everything was well thought-out. The Russian guests were introduced in order of rank by the Byzantine courtiers. They strolled ceremoniously through the great palace, passed through gardens and halls, until they finally came to a halt before the Emperor and Empress in Justinian's triclinium, where thrones of gold stood on a dais covered with purple silk. Organs and wind instruments were on hand to lend festivity to the entry. It was magnificent to behold the presentations and the exchanges of expressions of esteem. The same day a banquet had been arranged in the triclinium: 'The Empress and the Consort to the heir apparent had taken their places on the above-mentioned thrones, and the Princess had stationed herself beside it. When the other princesses had been introduced in order of rank by the master of ceremonies, and when they had bowed to the ground, the Princess inclined her head slightly and sat down at the place where she stood, at her own table with her ladies-in-waiting in order of rank. In the Golden Palace another banquet was taking place. Eating there were all the envoys from the Russian Grand Duke, the Princess's escort and relatives, together with the merchants, and they received: her nephew, 30 *miliarenses;* eight near relatives, 20 *miliarenses* each; forty-three merchants, 12 *miliarenses* each; the priest Gregory, 8 *miliarenses;* Sviatolav's escort, 5 *miliarenses* each; six persons among the envoy's company, 3 *miliarenses* each; the Princess's interpreter, 15 *miliarenses.* To the Princess 500 *miliarenses* were handed on a gold plate; to six women standing near her, 20 *miliarenses;* and to eighteen servant girls, 8 *miliarenses* each.' In this manner magnificent feasts succeeded each other with yet more money for the highly-esteemed guests, whose complaisant attitude and admiration for this splendid arrangement ought to have increased considerably.

With trade negotiations and gifts the Rus were glad to settle with the Byzantines. Terrifying weapons, such as the Greek fire, which was spewed out at the enemy, had made hostile visits less attractive than diplomatic ones. At any rate, the wealth of Constantinople was surrounded by a glow of adventure, which made enlistment in the Varangian Guard something particularly glorious.

As everywhere else in foreign countries where the Norsemen settled down amongst the original population, they easily merged into the customs of the people and married into their families. The Vikings

An exotic feature in the Nordic Viking era is this Arabian brazier of bronze, found at Hamrånge, Gästrikland, Sweden. It presumably once heated a house in Serkland, but in the north, where it came to rest after a long journey, one had an open fireplace in the middle of the floor, and there it must have seemed very peculiar. 40 cms. high. Gävle Museum, Sweden.

became burghers, farmers, nobles and kings. Russia gradually became—as appears from city finds, including, amongst other things, birch-bark inscriptions—strongly marked by Byzantium. But it always had personal links with Scandinavia. As late as the middle of the 11th century a band of Vikings from central Sweden made their way east to the Volga and on to Serkland, the beckoning land of silk and adventure beyond the Caspian Sea. It ended in tragedy. One after the other, they fell. The close-knit band shrank as they struggled on. The wealth, the far-off goal, was only a mirage; the silver mines had long since been worked out. The leader, Ingvar, was only 25 years old. Left was the memory of those who were bitterly missed. Over them stand the remains of twenty-four rune-stones. One of them reads: 'Anvid and Gisle and Kar and Bläse and Djärv, they raised this stone after Gunlev, their father. He fell in the east with Ingvar. God help his soul.' It is a remarkable thought that these last Vikings were Christians. In the idiom of the time they were called 'prey of the eagles.'

We have a reflection of Ingvar's expedition, fantastic and incredible, in a saga; but the most palpable memory of Swedish expeditions stands in runes at Gripsholm. It is cut in stone, and is not easily forgotten:

> They fared like men
> Afar after gold
> And in the east
> Gave the eagle food.
> They died to the south
> In Serkland.

The double-edged sword was a cruel and effective instrument in the hands of the Vikings. The sword-blades were often made up of a flexible centre-piece with welded-on hard edges. The hilts have inlays of precious metals. The swords, which are in the State Historical Museum, Stockholm, are from the left, finds from Lunda in Uppland, Överjärna in Södermanland, Järfälla in Uppland, and Birka in Lake Mälar.

An Historical Cross-Section

A survey of the Viking expeditions easily gives the impression that each of the Nordic peoples had its own goal, and that the emigrants were soon absorbed into the foreign peoples.

This is a simplification. Many great men travelled far and wide. They sought riches and honour wherever they were to be found. To name only one example: Harald Hardrade had to fly to Gardarike when he was very young. From there he made his way to Constantinople and became in time Commander of the Varangian Guard. He will have acquired then a certain knowledge of languages. In 1046 he headed back to Norway, obtained a share of royal power and later became sole king. Twenty years after that he undertook the fateful attack on England, when he fell at Stamford Bridge, near York. His first wife was the daughter of Prince Jaroslav; he was later married to a Norsewoman.

Politically contracted marriages were, on the whole, universal. Family ties were strong and carried obligations. Nordic families abroad could hold their own for generation after generation, and maintained links with their homeland. From there they could get support and sometimes sent for women. Ivar's dynasty, whose ancestor had been king in Dublin, can thus be followed through the centuries; rulers succeeded each other and lived up to their fathers' fame, sometimes in mutual competition. Ivar's sons Sigfrid and Sigtryg defended themselves against Halvdan, but then turned against each other. Sigtryg became sole king and invaded England. The energetic Ragnvald became the next great name of Ivar's line. Later came Olav Kvaran, great and contentious, rich in victories. His sister was married to Olav Tryggvason. But he too finally suffered defeat and went into a monastery. We still hear of Ivar's descendants at the end of the century.

In this way families branched out. The Vikings reconnoitred everywhere for fresh opportunities. The first Norseman in Iceland that we know by name was Gardar, of Swedish descent. He owned land in Zealand, was married to a woman from Sudrö and emigrated to Iceland. Several Swedish rune-stones mention England, for example the Väsby inscription: 'Ale had this stone raised to his own

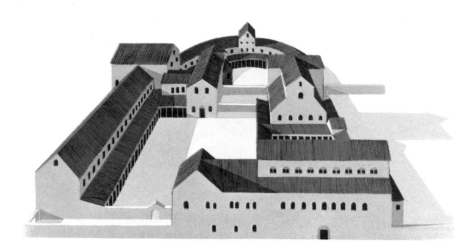

memory. He took Canute's geld in England. God help his soul.' Or the Grinda stone in Södermanland: 'Grytgård, Enride—the sons—made to father bold. Gudve was in the west of England, geld he divided. Strongholds in Saxland he attacked like a man.'

We do not know if Rolf (Rollo), the conqueror of Normandy, was of Danish or Norwegian descent. This was hardly of decisive importance for his warriors. Nationality was a vague concept compared to the brotherhood of arms, family and home locality.

The circumstances in Ireland are characteristic. To all appearances Danish and Norwegian Vikings stood opposed to one another, but this was due to the fact that the latter had come from the north, via the Scottish islands, and the Danes from England. It was not long before alliances were made lengthwise and crosswise, and also with Irish chieftains. How this functioned can be seen by following the political game of the powerful chieftains. People grouped themselves about them without constraint.

The amazing span of the Viking journeys appears from a few suitably chosen dates from their 250 years.

829—839. The Vikings were active from Russia to Iceland. In Wessex King Egbert tried to defend himself against minor attacks by Viking fleets. In 829, at Ingelheim, the imperial castle near Mainz, Ansgar met the exiled Danish King Harald. They travelled northwards, and after Ansgar had received a noteworthy ship from the Bishop of Cologne, the King kept the missionary company.

Ten years later, other Norsemen came to Ingelheim, envoys of Swedish nationality from the ruler of a kingdom in Russia, on their way home after a visit to Constantinople.

The Imperial Palace at Ingelheim was the meeting-place on several occasions for Vikings and the powerful ones of the western continent. Here the Danish King Harald associated with Ansgar, and here a delegation from northern Russia paid a visit on their way home.

The representation of Louis the Pious, a son of Charlemagne, might almost be an illustration to the discussion he held with his advisers about the foreign members of the Byzantine delegation which came to him at Ingelheim in 839. These foreigners asserted that they were of Swedish nationality, and that they represented the kingdom (khaganate) of the Rus. This information, which we have from Bishop Prudentius, gives us no further details about this kingdom. After a contemporary drawing.

In the same year, the Norwegian sea-king Thorgisl landed in Ireland, where he—and his wife—created scandal in the monasteries and spread fear about them.

Prudentius writes, full of dark forebodings, in prophetic style: 'The heathens shall come in numerous ships upon you and the greater part of the Christians' land and people, and they will lay waste all your property with fire and sword.' Dorestad was plundered, and Danes settled on islands at the mouth of the Thames. A Danish king, Horik, and a Swede, Bern, are mentioned.

In 872 the sea-battle at Havrsfjord was fought. Harald Harfagri made himself ruler over Norway and took over, amongst other things, the tax revenues. Eminent men emigrated across the Atlantic. He completed his victories by placing under him the Earldom of the Orkney Islands. The Danes settled in England. Ivar proclaimed himself king over the Northmen in Ireland and in Britain. The Vikings conquered Angers, moved their wives and children there from an island in the Loire, and opened a market in the town.

In 911 Rollo received Normandy as a province from Charles the Simple, and was baptised the following year. The Anglo-Saxon King Edward and his energetic sister Ethelfleda secured their position by driving back the Vikings. The Northumberland Vikings suffered defeat at Tettenham. On the Caspian Sea and in southern Russia Norsemen plundered. The following year a treaty was concluded between the envoys of the Grand Duke of the Rus (with Nordic names such as Karl, Ingeld and Torolf) and the two Emperors of Byzantium on the legal relations between the peoples in the event of manslaughter, stranded ships, etc.

In 937 the Vikings suffered a defeat at Brunanburh Athelstan (with the help of other Vikings) became ruler over the greater part of England. The last Swedish ruler in South Jutland abandoned his dominion. Hakon Adelstensfoster (who grew up with the Anglo-Saxon king) assumed authority in Norway. He made the Goths in west Sweden pay tax, introduced laws and organised provincial defence.

In 974 Otto II attacked Denmark and captured Hedeby. King Harald (baptised about 960) seized power in southern Norway. Earl Hakon held the north of Norway. The Swedish King Erik Segersäll defeated the Vikings who attacked Uppsala. Birka completely lost its importance during these years. The Baltic east coast was brought under King Harald.

In 1000 Sven Forkbeard defeated his former companion-in-arms from England, Olav Tryggvason, in the sea-battle at Svolder. Leif the Lucky voyaged to Vinland from the Greenland settlements. The Icelandic Althing adopted Christianity.

In 1035 Knut the Great (Canute) died, and his North Sea kingdom

HELLULAND

GREENLAND

MARKLAND

Sandnes

Brattahlid⁷⁴

Herjolfsnes

ARCTIC CIRCLE

ICELAND

Snæfellsnes

Thingvalla¹⁷⁹

VINLAND

Faeroes

Shetland Islands⁴²

Jarlshof⁴⁰

Orkney Islan

Lindisfarn

THE WORLD OF THE VIKINGS

stretched from Newfoundland in the west to the Caspian
Sea in the east, ca. 8,000 km., and from the Arctic
Ocean to Baghdad in the south, ca. 4,000 km.

The numerals which occur in the map after certain place-
names indicate pages in the book with illustrations from
these places.

Man²³⁰

York

Dublin

London

Skellig⁴⁶

Rou

Loire

Tou

important Viking journeys

important caravan routes

0   500   1000   1500 Kms.

Lisbon

Gudalquivir

Cordova

Cadiz

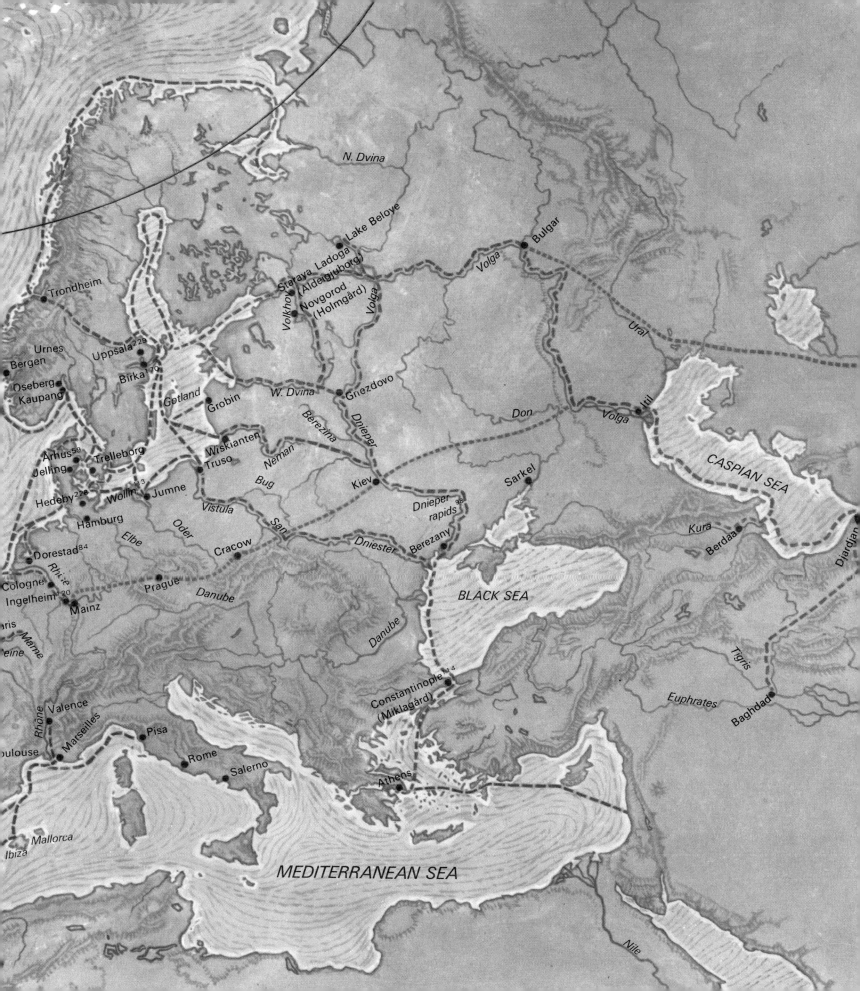

Trondheim

Urnes
Bergen

Oseberg
Kaupang

Uppsala[229]

Birka[70]

Gotland

Grobin

Árhus[59]

Trelleborg

Jelling

Wiskianten

Truso

Hedeby[228]

Wollin[113]

Jumne

Hamburg

Dorestad[84]

Cologne

Rhine

Ingelheim[120]

Mainz

Paris

Marne

Seine

Valence

Rhône

Marseilles

Toulouse

Pisa

Rome

Salerno

Mallorca

Ibiza

Staraya Ladoga
(Aldeigjuborg)

Volkhov

Novgorod
(Holmgård)

Lake Beloye

N. Dvina

Bulgar

Volga

Volga

Volga

Ural

W. Dvina

Gnezdovo

Berezina

Dnieper

Neman

Bug

Kiev

Don

Volga

Itil

Sarkel

CASPIAN SEA

Kura

Berdaa

Djardjan

Vistula

Oder

Elbe

Cracow

San

Prague

Danube

Dniester

Berezany

Dnieper
rapids[98]

BLACK SEA

Danube

Constantinople[144]
(Miklagård)

Athens

Tigris

Euphrates

Baghdad

Nile

MEDITERRANEAN SEA

Carved head of a predatory animal in wood, found in the River Schelde. It was either the figure-head of a Viking ship or decoration for a 'high-seat.' British Museum, London.

A duel, detail on a Gotland picture-stone from Smiss in När.

fell apart. The Faeroe Islands had to pay tax to Norway. The Viking era gradually faded out.

Most of the sources for the history of the Viking era stem from men of the Church. Their opinions and antipathies have left their mark on the accounts. These are full of unverifiable assertions. Amongst themselves, too, the writers from the great ecclesiastical foundations disputed with each other, and worded their historical works so that their own sect stood in the best possible light. Everyday life appeared only exceptionally, though we have vivid glimpses from biographies such as Ansgar's. A matter that is hard to estimate is, for example, social conditions, since the royal power, the position of the chieftains, etc., underwent changes during the course of the Viking era and the period that followed, which was when most of the sources were written down and received their form. On the whole, many words hold strange concepts, which are foreign to us. In those days they had a quite different background and application, which with care can be reconstructed from the context of the words. Honour implied self-vindication, and this demanded revenge on those who violated one's self-esteem. Behind this lay the unity of the family, both between the living and with vanished generations. If anyone was declared to be without honour, he was placed outside these mutual bonds and became a miscreant. So that this should not happen and react on the family, he had to demand revenge and vindicate his honour.

What we should call luck was a concrete idea to a Norsemen, an attribute: to have a favourable wind when sailing, victory in battle, success on a hazardous journey. A man's protective spirit, his *hamingja*, acted also through other people. A king with this special luck gave the country good harvests. His power and influence were of the same kind as the common man's, but greater.

People could participate in the king's *hamingja* in order thereby to carry out an exploit or win a victory. But if it failed, if the people had to undergo year after year of bad crops and bad luck, then this was the king's fault and it was best to get rid of him.

Viking Society

There is reason to consider whether the form of their society served as a curb or a spur to the Norsemen's activity. In itself an emigration need be no more than a conveyance to another place. Problems arose, however, when they met other forms of society; since the individual was to such a high degree a part of his family, it might be thought that he found it hard to accept forms of society that conflicted with family feelings. This could happen in the towns, which were beginning to grow up just at that time in the north.

Although the Vikings abroad gave out that they were all equal, there were important distinctions nonetheless, not least between slaves and freemen. The rune-stones, and the graves with very rich or poor decoration, tell as clearly as contemporary foreign sources of kings, chieftains, free warriors, women, smiths and ship-owners, freedmen, slaves, etc. Often enough it is the men who are given prominence, but a woman had such prestige that she could equally well raise a grave-stone over her husband as a son over his father. She held her own for the most part in a discreet way, but was respected and influential.

Within the great families ambition and self-assertion might develop violently. It was not easy for kings to make themselves felt, surrounded as they were by power-conscious chieftains—some even of their own family. If the chieftains could afford to they kept a hird, larger or smaller, all according to their landed property and the wealth they squeezed from people. But it was an anxiety to pay a standing army, and in addition the fleet had to be organized by levy, which followed an order for common defence or attack, but which was controlled by the chieftains. It took a strong personality to govern a lot of self-willed chieftains, and right up to the end of the Viking era there were plenty of them. To this must be added the limitation which the free peasantry, gathered at the Thing, imposed on a ruler's freedom of action.

The first Nordic king who left any memoirs behind him—albeit in lapidary form—was Harald Bluetooth: he united Denmark and Norway, made the Danes Christian, and raised the great memorials over his parents which are still preserved today; he seemed strong, but he still ended his days in exile, at Jumne on the island of Wollin, which he had conquered.

If we imagine that his predecessor, Gottfrid, had raised a memorial in the years just after 800, this would have been no less impressive. He fortified the country with a wall from the Baltic to the North Sea, unified Denmark and Norway (southern Norway), moved the inhabitants from the town of Reric to his own, Hedeby (Sliestorp) and led an attack to the south to protect the country against Charlemagne and the impenitent Slavs.

With his sudden death—he was killed by a man from his hird— the position of the country was weakened. In both cases, of Gottfrid and of Harald, the achievement of the king was decisive, and the qualities of his successor were of corresponding importance. His luck and his protective spirit, his *hamingja,* stood behind victories and fertility. So sacrifices were made to the king for good years. In Sweden this took place once a year in Uppsala, and the same occurred

The eminent man out hunting. On his left hand sits the falcon ready to obey his master's command; in front, the hounds chase after prey. In more cultivated districts, hunting was undoubtedly controlled by chieftains and kings, but in the large areas in the north it was free. Detail from the Bayeux tapestry.

presumably each year in the other Nordic lands.

Amongst the rulers, mutual alliances were made now and then, which were occasionally sealed by marriage. Connected families naturally had to support one another, and this made constellations of power develop and change with amazing consequences. Thus Sven Forkbeard rejected his wife Gunhild and married Sigrid Storrad, the widow of his former enemy, the Swedish King Erik Segersäll. He received as companion the Norwegian Earl Hakon's son Erik, who married Sven's daughter Gyda. Together they turned on Olav Tryggvason, Sven's former companion in arms on the expedition to England of 994—95. The latter had tried in vain to secure his position by marrying Sven's sister Tyra, who had fled from her Polish husband Boleslav. One chose the family ties that were politically the most valuable, or else one let oneself be ruled by passion. Sigrid was evidently full of hatred for Olav. The three allies, Sven, Erik and their relative Olof Skötkonung of Sweden, attacked Olav Tryggvason when he was on his way to collect Tyra's dowry and defeated him at Svolder in the year 1000. Other, random examples of alliances being made and sealed can also be found. Thus on the great rune-stone in Sönder Vissing, Jutland, we learn that King Harald Bluetooth was married to Tova, the daughter of the Slavic King Mistivoy. This is only *one* example of how the Nordic kings sought to collaborate with the Slavic princes to the south and east of Scandinavia.

The kings ruled just as much over people as over territories. Since not all of a king's sons could inherit the power, they sometimes came

The proudest rune-stone of the north was raised by King Harald Bluetooth at Jelling over his parents. It has hardly been moved substantially from its place by the present church, between the two upthrusting burial-mounds, 8.5 and 11.0 m. high. Together with the stone of his father, King Gorm, to his wife Tyra, it formed part of a magnificent grave-monument. Two rows of *bautastenar*, which at one end are crowned by the southern mound, except for the outermost part, enclosed the central section. To judge by similar constructions from this period, this is undoubtedly a

matter of a mighty ship-setting, which may have reached right to the northern mound. The great Jelling stone has pictorial representations on two sides, of Christ and of the lion struggling with the snake, which are discussed on p. 200. On the three sides the following inscription may be read: 'King Harald had this stone raised after Gorm his father and Tyra his mother, that Harald who won the whole of Denmark and Norway for himself and made the Danes Christians.' The stone is 2.4 m. high.

into conflict with each other, but it could equally well happen that one of them sought a kingdom for himself abroad. This was the way the Swedish dominion in south Jutland was founded, which lasted for three generations. We know this from rune-stones, amongst other things. The first king, Olof, appears around 900 in the important area in the very south of Jutland, where the merchants met at Hedeby and the routes converged. During the years between 900 and c. 940, when first the son Gnupa, and after him the grandson Sigtryg held sway, the family maintained its domination in order to yield then to the Danish king.

It was no doubt in the same manner that a Swedish dynasty seized power in a part of Russia. With the help of stalwart bands they made sure of key positions, but the fate of the family was shaped by the country's vast proportions. Just as the Swedish rulers in South Jutland took Danish consorts—Gnupa's wife was a daughter of Odinkar, certainly a chieftain—the Swedish Viking kings secured their position with queens from the Slavic ruling families.

The king derived an income from his estates and from conquests. The first share of the booty went to him. On his estates he had administrators, and he could travel from farm to farm and receive maintenance for himself and his large following.

But it was natural that the king should seek other means to enable him to pay his hird and exercise a better control over the country's great chieftains—not to mention the men of the Thing. He wanted to have professional soldiers, at any rate people who were prepared to subordinate themselves for a time. They came forward abundantly, and we read on the rune-stones how people from Sweden, for example, took part in the Danish king's conquest of England. Some lost their lives already in Denmark during the preparations, amongst them perhaps the Sven whose memory is commemorated on the stone at Husby-Lyhundra in Uppland: 'He died in Jutland. He was to go to England.' For a mounted army to be used to best effect, it had to be trained intensively, otherwise the right effect was not achieved. The cavalry force of the late Viking era, supported by bowmen, was a finely-tuned instrument when it was well drilled.

Against this background one can understand the carefully planned circular fortresses in Denmark: Trelleborg, Nonnebakken, Fyrkat and Aggersborg. They were specially designed as barracks for regular troops, who at the same time kept a check on the powerful provincial chieftain and made sure that he remained loyal.

From these fortresses, which lay on important key-passages, other things, too, were watched over in the life of the community. Nonnebakken at Odense kept an eye on the town for the power-holder, who can hardly have been other than the king himself. Through these well-built fortresses he gained influence around the country.

The power-holder needed considerable means to maintain such barracks—in Aggersborg alone fully 3,000 men, in Trelleborg a third as many. And just as such troops were valuable to the skilful, wealthy leader, so too were they dangerous for the one who could not give them suitable provisions. They knew extremely well how to wring money from conquered territories; they were men who headed for home like the later gold-diggers, and bragged about how they had got the king's money in England. They could say that they belonged to the ones who had manfully stormed the English cities. A glitter of riches hung about these bold men. Only with ever-flowing sources of wealth could such large forces be maintained, otherwise they became more of a risk than a help. To have too many in the vicinity of a royal estate, with women and goods, was not advisable. The troops belonged at home where they could be used and where they could be trained. So long as they contributed to the acquisition of income, in the widest sense of the word, one was also in a position to pay them.

These warriors live on in the sagas in romantic guise, as *Jomsvikings*. Here is all that posterity could wish for in the way of valiant and dauntless fighters, who take leave of their turbulent lives with a last, well-turned retort.

Far closer to the truth is the connection between the men of the round-forts and the Tingslid and its law, the 'Vederlag.' The latter regulated the duties of the warriors to their master and their mutual position. The soldiers—like the forts—were divided into quarters, and they had their own court, a sort of Thing.

It was obviously these men who were commemorated on the rune-stones as 'fighters,' good and brave, or as chieftains, 'thanes,' and leaders. Many of them kept together as foster-brothers and are sometimes called brothers, without there being any kinship with those who raised the stone. Amongst those who served Sven Forkbeard was Erik, 'who met his death when the warriors set about (besieged) Hedeby, and he was a *styrman,* a very high-born warrior.' Leaders like Erik could be comrades with the other warriors. An intimate solidarity easily arose between these men, when they endured challenging dangers side by side and were sometimes saved by a comrade. This can be seen on the Hällestad stone: 'Eskil set up this

The Viking fortress of Fyrkat, on the Kattegatt side of north Jutland, lay well protected by low-lying ground on three sides and with an open view over the glen and the river, which at that time was wider. The fortress lay where the north-south route along the east coast of Jutland crossed the east-west passage through the valley to the coast.

131

stone after Toke, Gorm's son, his gracious lord. He fled not at Uppsala. Warriors raised to their brother (i.e. foster-brother) the stone on the hill; firm it stands with runes. They went nearest Gorm's son Toke.' A proud memorial to bravery. Many fell there 'while they had weapons.'

But the king needed other assistants besides commanders and administrators. In the towns he had both tax revenues and obligations to look after. He had to have his representative there, who could organize help in case of attack and collect the monies which were due to the ruler, amongst others, undoubtedly a tax on house-property (which we hear about in the very earliest town charters), and various fees, e.g. from the markets. The towns were a source of income in the same way as the conquered territories, where earls looked after the king's affairs.

Within the actual Nordic lands, there were earls for provincial regions in the middle of the 11th century, as we know from the border-treaty between the Danish and Swedish kings. Three earls came from Jutland, one from Zealand, one from Skåne, and one from Halland; while from Sweden, six earls (including one from Östergötland) came to the meeting.

These great men, especially during the earlier period, were virtually independent. In Denmark and Iceland they combined, like the king,

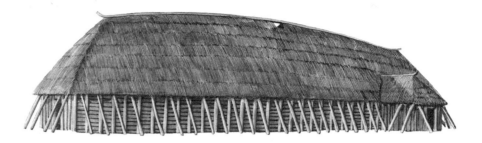

Like the other Viking fortresses, Fyrkat had a strict geometrical plan, left. The circle which the rampart describes is divided into quarter-sections by crossing roads about 120 m. long, and in each was a group of four 'barracks.' These were 28.5 m. long, constructed with a mixture of post-house and wattle-and-daub technique, with buttressed walls and a roof of thatch or shingles. They had three rooms: a room at each end and a large hall in the centre with exits at two diagonal corners for a quick turn-out. The roads, including the ring-way within the rampart, were paved with wood. The rampart had a wooden parapet which also ran over the gates.

Right, an attempt to reconstruct one of the houses in the Fyrkat fortress. It appears from sections through the post-holes that the outer posts went down obliquely and obviously buttressed the large, heavy roof, the weight of which rested mainly on the two inner rows of vertical posts. The entrance was built out slightly. The smoke-hole is visible in the middle of the roof-ridge.

Left centre, coin from Birka, adapted as an amulet. This side shows the picture of a house, which is of particular interest since one can see the obliquely-set outer posts that buttress the roof—thus far one may now venture to interpret this simple representation. Animal-heads adorn the gables. It may well be the same type of house as those at Fyrkat and Trelleborg. Ca. 2.5 cms. in diameter. The Coin Cabinet, Stockholm.

Below, well-armed men, perhaps sent on a commission by the chieftain, who sits on his 'high-seat.' Picture-stone from Buttle, Änge, Gotland.

a religious and a secular authority. They were both *gode* (heathen priest) and chieftain *(thegn)* for the hird. One called Alle is known to us through the memorial-stone of his wife, Ragnhild, in Glavendrup on North Fyn. She had, moreover, been married once before, in South Zealand to Gunnulv, whose heathen disposition she proclaims and ends: 'Few were born better than he.' With her second husband, Alle, the eloquent lady lived on North Fyn, to which she came after her marriage. Both times she had got high-born and prominent husbands. She was well aware of this and did not forget it when the obituary was to be composed.

The king, as one can well imagine, stood in tense relationship with the chieftains, who often felt themselves his equals. Ottar, whom we have already met, was just such an independent north-Norwegian chieftain, who added to his income from his estate and business activities by levying a tax on the Lapps in his district, which will have been great. Shortly after, the Norwegian King, Harald Harfagri, set himself over the independence of the Norwegian chieftains, when he united Norway around 872, and requisitioned the tax on his own account.

It is small wonder that there was friction in the relationship between the king and the highest in the society. It explains some strange manipulations on the part of the king, not always easy to penetrate. One suspects that the atmosphere from time to time was gloomy and thundery. The king followed with suspicion the movements of his great men, their meetings with each other, their attempts to become popular with the people, their prosperous forays and advantageous marriages, for themselves and those nearest to them. Often enough these suspicions proved to be well-founded. Even his own son might give him cause to feel uncertain, though most of the young men waited patiently for their time to succeed. King Harald Bluetooth had to fly to Wollin, badly wounded, after the battle with his far more successful son Sven, the renowned war-leader. Canute the Great caused his brother-in-law Ulf to be killed and looked kindly upon his English earl, Godevin (a kinsman of Ulf); and not without reason as it later turned out, when he represented English interests. Without loyal helpers, the king—and the earl—was badly off, though seldom as badly as in the Byzantine Empire. In the North, after all, the lifeguards were made up of Northmen, not of foreigners. One of the highest in his suite was the master of the stables; like the marshal in southern lands, he was originally responsible for the horses. Although this was in itself a responsible post, it led to greater influence, and the master of the stables sometimes represented his lord. Lower in rank was the master mariner, who directed the king's vessels, and the thane, who led his hird of freemen. The latter for their part honoured their master, who looked after them well.

A more sporadic attachment was that of the *skald,* or court poet, and the artist-craftsman. It was a sure foundation for fame to have one's exploits delivered in sonorous, artful words which already fixed themselves in the memory the first time the poem was recited. The cunning rhythms bound the words together with a magic power, so that they could not be altered without the poem dying. We know many *skalds,* several from Iceland, and we have already cited Sigvat, Saint Olav's faithful companion. We shall meet others later in the chapter on Profiles of Artists.

For the great man, it was no less essential to have beautiful equipment and beautiful objects about him. House, household goods and ship, wagons and sledges, were made conspicuous with elegant carvings. One recognized a man by his noble belongings and one admired his wife, who wore rare and costly jewels. They enchanted the eye, gleaming with gold and silver, designed in stylized animal-patterns. Every woman wanted to have such beautiful brooches and rings, even if they were only of bronze or—better still—gilded, so that one thought they were of gold. But for the keen observer quality was a criterion.

One could not mistake the king or the earl. If the king came riding by, one saw how the light flashed on the gilded mountings of his harness, and one was dazzled by the finely inlaid weapons and helmets. Their love of splendour appears in the equipment in the graves of the great and in the equivalent women's graves. The noble lady who was buried in the Oseberg ship—can she have been other than a queen?—had exquisite taste and such renowned riches that they were not allowed to lie in peace. Eager robbers tore some of the arm-bones from the corpse to get at the rings. The heathen generations went into the world of the dead as well equipped as in life. They also had with them their usual assistant, a slave, so that they were not alone in the many situations in which they normally received help. Otherwise, how would they get along? In life they were surrounded by slaves and freedmen, in the kitchen and stable, in the fields and meadows, and in all the other occupations.

Harness-mounts of gilded bronze from Broa, Halla, Gotland. These pieces exhibit both originality and a fine style. The animal-motifs are typical of Gotland art; some of them are seen as if through round panes. The two at the top are shaped like the head of a beast of prey, while the rectangular mounts are crowned with plastic animal-heads. The large rectangular mounts are ca. 9 cms. high, the smaller one 6 cms. State Historical Museum, Stockholm.

A reconstruction based on preserved fragments of a Viking helmet from Gjermundbu in Norway. The crown is round, not pointed, as one otherwise often sees in pictures from the period. It is solid, wrought of iron plates and particularly strong at the parts around the eyes and nose.

loyal, and they in their turn had to be well regarded by their crew. Without victories and rich booty one could expect mutiny.

The farmers, the backbone of the social community, also manned the ships. They were occupied normally not only with agriculture and stock-raising, smithy-work and carpentry for household needs, but also sometimes went off on Viking expeditions. It was these men who met at the Thing. It was their taste and purchasing power that were decisive for the professional craftsmen, who provided the market with the highly-esteemed types of ornament in simple, mass-produced forms. Only the high-born women could allow themselves the satisfaction of artistic and original handiwork.

The farmer was head of the family, but his wife in her quiet way had no less influence. She could raise a memorial-stone over her

In this drinking scene from the Bayeux tapestry one can see that both goblets as well as beautifully mounted drinking-horns were put to use.

husband just as well as he over her. She took over the inheritance when the male heirs fell away. This was no rare occurrence in those unruly times. On the whole, one gets no impression that they lived in large families when one reads the runic inscriptions on the grave-stones. In Hansta, Uppland, lived two brothers, Gärdar and Jorund. They inherited their father's farm, but went off like so many others on a voyage to Byzantium, where they died. Their mother took over the property, and after her death it went to her two brothers.

Large estates arose through the amalgamation of several properties. In Nora, Uppland, Finnvid's two sons had a farm jointly, which—according to their own way of expressing it—was their *odal* (joint inheritance) and family property. One of them, Olev, was treacherously killed on Finnheden (now Finnveden). The other, Björn, raised a memorial-stone over him at the main farm in Älgesta, some way from Nora. The boundary of the property was fixed by boundary-stones, which is mentioned in runic inscriptions.

A simple family saga, even scantier than the Icelandic ones, but realistic, is carved on a rock at Hillersjö, Uppland. 'Germund married Gerlög, when she was a maiden. Later they had a son, before Germund was drowned. The son died later. Then she married Gudrik. They had children. Of these only a girl lived; she was called Inga. Ragnfast of Snottsta married her. Afterwards he died, and their son after him. And the mother inherited from her son. Inga afterwards married Erik. Then she died. Then Gerlög inherited from Inga, her daughter.' The family kept the farm, as appears from this description, when the right of inheritance could not be denied. The heritage went from father to son, or from son to mother, until the grand-mother was left sitting resignedly with the family's property. On some occasions, as in Nora, two brothers are mentioned as joint

Beautiful mounts of gilded bronze adorn the drinking-horn from Århus. The horn itself has vanished but is reconstructed in the drawing. The decoration consists of an elegant bird-frieze in the late Viking style. Ca. 8 cms. wide. National Museum, Copenhagen.

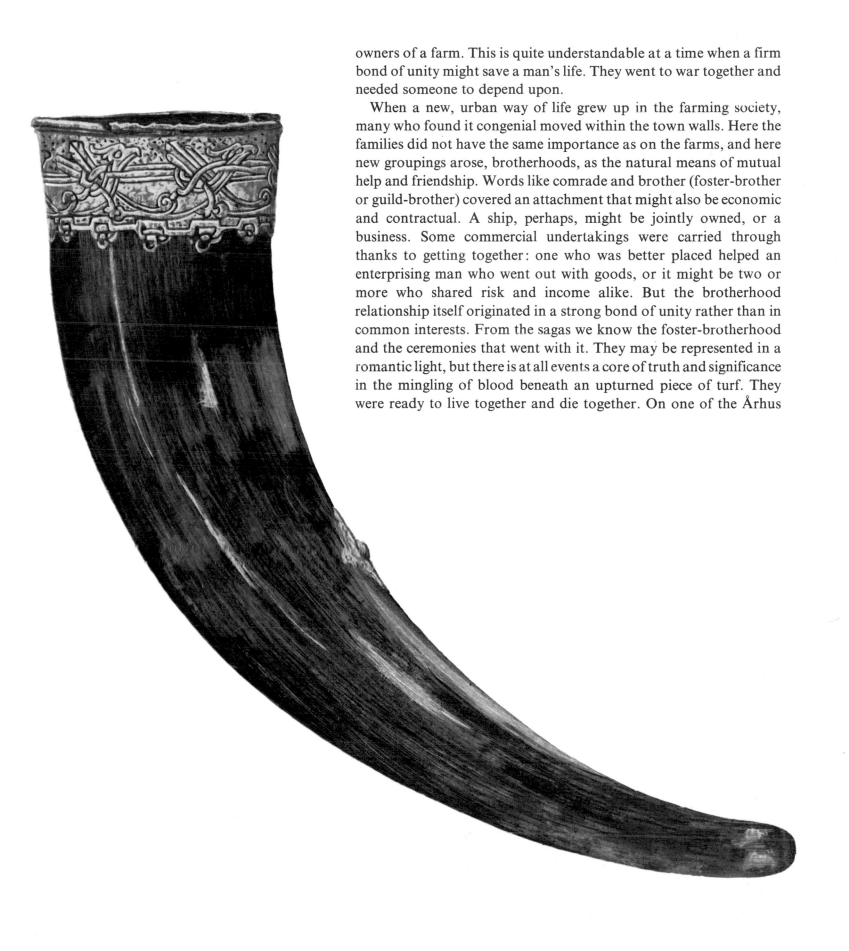

owners of a farm. This is quite understandable at a time when a firm bond of unity might save a man's life. They went to war together and needed someone to depend upon.

When a new, urban way of life grew up in the farming society, many who found it congenial moved within the town walls. Here the families did not have the same importance as on the farms, and here new groupings arose, brotherhoods, as the natural means of mutual help and friendship. Words like comrade and brother (foster-brother or guild-brother) covered an attachment that might also be economic and contractual. A ship, perhaps, might be jointly owned, or a business. Some commercial undertakings were carried through thanks to getting together: one who was better placed helped an enterprising man who went out with goods, or it might be two or more who shared risk and income alike. But the brotherhood relationship itself originated in a strong bond of unity rather than in common interests. From the sagas we know the foster-brotherhood and the ceremonies that went with it. They may be represented in a romantic light, but there is at all events a core of truth and significance in the mingling of blood beneath an upturned piece of turf. They were ready to live together and die together. On one of the Århus

stones one can read of three men who raised a stone over their comrade, who, remarkably enough, owned a ship with a fifth named man (not with the comrades).

The children of the family were examined by the father immediately after birth. He might decide that a child was to be put out, if it was deformed or in any other way had no prospect of getting along. Its upbringing was sometimes given over to a foster-father of lower class, perhaps a slave; nevertheless, close ties were established between child and foster-father. We also hear of a child being sent away to a friend's family to be brought up with them. Children who were brought together in this way during their growing years might conclude a foster-brotherhood.

Class distinctions, not least in homes where bond and high-born associated freely with each other, could be obliterated, and deserving slaves were sometimes given their freedom. There are rune-stones which give proof of this. In gratitude the freedman raised a memorial to his dead master, like Toke the smith, who raised a stone in Hörning, near Århus, to Troels Gudmundsson, who gave him gold and salvation (money and freedom).

Although we read time after time assertions by the Vikings that they were all equal, most of the sources reveal the existence of significant class distinctions. During an attack abroad, a band of Norsemen may have felt themselves equally placed, but this was not always open to them in the ordered conditions at home. A glance at some of the graves from the Viking period soon convinces one of this. The mighty barrows and stone-erections of King Gorm and

The Mammen axe, found in north Jutland, is one of the finest works of art in the style that took its name from this find, Mammen. On this side of the axe one can see a bird of elegant curves with a heavy triangular body and spiral-shaped thighs. The limbs are in the form of acanthus creeper. National Museum, Copenhagen.

This beautiful standing stone is adorned with leaf-creeper and animal-motifs, which were in fashion just after the year 1000. It was set up to Asser Saxe, who was clearly a prominent citizen of Århus. On two sides of the stone one may read: 'Toste and Hove together with Frebjörn raised this stone after Asser Saxe, their comrade, a very well-born churl. He died the greatest non-villain among men; he owned ships together with Arne.' Prehistoric Museum, Moesgård, Århus. 1.6 m. high.

King Harald in Jelling were constructed by a ruling family with access to a labour force. The proud words of the son to his parents leave no room for doubt: 'King Harald had these cairns (grave-memorials) made after his father Gorm and his mother Tyra, that Harald who won the whole of Denmark and Norway for himself, and who made the Danes Christians.' The great burial-chamber in one of the barrows and some finds left there by chance reveal a milieu which we know better from Oseberg and Röd in Norway.

The Nordic sea-kings who ravaged in foreign lands sometimes found their last resting-place there, one of them in Île de Groix off Brittany, where only a few finds from the grave are left; others—of Swedish family—were buried in their conquered realm in South Jutland, near Hedeby. Yet another, a Dane, received a simple yet impressive grave-mound at Kalmarsund on Öland. The inscription on the Karlevi stone moves in rhythms that make us think of an Icelandic *skald* as author of this obituary tribute to a great man, whose conquests are otherwise unknown to us: 'This stone is raised after Sibbe the Good, Foldar's son . . . Hidden lies he who was followed by the greatest deeds (this would be known to most), toiler for the goddess of war (chieftain) in this mound. Never shall more right-minded, battle-strong wagon-god (ship's captain) of the sea-king's mighty ground (the sea) hold sway over land in Denmark.'

The whole society finds its voice on the grave-stones; runes are carved by comrades over their friends, by the free farmer over his father or wife, or she raised a memorial to honour her mate; master mariners, bailiffs, thanes, masters of the stables, Varangian and Viking, *thule* (sorcerer?) and *gode* (heathen priest), the smith, the rune-cutter and rune-painter; even the freedman is brought to our notice when we read the runic inscriptions. Only the humblest of all, the slave, does not exist. Nameless he lies in his grave. But the texts from the Viking period give us something more than a mere reflection of the society, of a clearly partitioned and yet simple world. The words from that period allow the tongue to repeat the original language. One notices a shift of meaning from then to now, a change in the cast of thought. The names alone take us back to a far-off and yet closely related time: Haraldr, Toki, Othinkor, Gnupa, Hakun, Kätil, Roulfr, Gunulfr. It becomes clear to one how the place-names sounded in their earlier forms, such as Hetabyr (Hedeby) and Norvägr (Norway); or the names of peoples, such as Iuti (Jutlanders) and Svear (Swedes). When we meet the poetry which came into being during Viking times, and which left its mark on some of the runic inscriptions, and the place-names which originated a thousand years ago, we get a remarkably vivid idea of the connection between that time and our own, both in its enduring features and in those that have changed.

The Farm

Scattered or in groups, the farms lay over the countryside. Slender columns of smoke rose from the middle of the roof-ridges and marked the site of a settlement from afar. The properties stretched across the fertile valleys and plains, trying to force back the wilderness and forest. Further away, in the hilly districts of Scandinavia, were outposts for seasonal grazing, hunting and iron-mining. Along the coasts, one lived by fishing, bird-catching and egg-collecting. Ice-runners, skates of bone, hung ready for the winter, so that with a spiked stick and a hook one could fish through a hole in the ice. The inhabitants were well able to work in wood or metal for household needs, but they required a number of raw materials, and luxury goods were much sought after. There was no shortage of people. The needs of the home could be supplied as to cloth, food and ale, but energy and plenty of land were necessary to secure a surplus of corn or meat. A good outlet for foodstuffs could be found among the town-dwellers engaged in specialized occupations, the craftsmen and merchants, or among the warrior bands—if these had not already got themselves food by brute force.

The houses left their mark on the countryside, but at the same time they merged into it, since they were constructed with the natural materials of the district: stone, turf, straw, wood and clay. The small farms consisted of only a single oblong house, rectangular or with bulging sides. It was sited so that the occupants had as little discomfort as possible from the prevailing wind. The large farms show obvious signs of having been added to, or of having consisted of several buildings. They also reveal the different strata of society. The great man naturally had a more spacious abode and a richer inventory than people in general. He had a hall in which to eat and feast, with 'high-seat pillars' so that everyone could see the place of the king or earl in the middle by the long fire. Stables, etc., were evidently separate from the dwelling-house, and there may have been a separate sleeping-room or sleeping-house. At any rate proper beds and bed-clothes were used in the environment of the great (see p. 150) and they took up rather a lot of room. Amongst ordinary people the place of honour was less evident, but a sort of high seat still marked the master's place, no doubt in a corner. These posts or props from the high seats accompanied an emigration and were thrown into the water off the foreign coast when a settlement was contemplated. Where the props drifted ashore, the house was built.

The ordinary farmer contented himself with a simple, oblong house

The Norwegian mountain-farm as it may have appeared, surrounded by little fields, stable and outhouses.

with an open hearth and low bunks along the walls at one end. The domestic animals were housed at the other. This helped to keep the cold away. For the great problem for the inhabitants was, of course, to keep warm. Nor were they spoiled for illumination: A shaft of light came down through the smoke-hole in the roof. Further light was obtained from simple lamps, known from the Oseberg grave, amongst other places, hemispherical iron bowls on a pole half a metre long. If one wanted more than light to manage by, one had to open the doors.

The Nordic countries are so dissimilar in nature that the mode of building was simply adapted to the surroundings. The climate of northern Scandinavia and Iceland, not to mention Greenland, demanded considerable insulation of the walls, a good deal more substantial than the Danish houses, though they too might need to be stopped up for the winter. In the northern countries turf and stones were piled up as a strong outer embankment or wall, and here the builders were lucky enough to have a kind of turf that was tough and well matted. But these rough layers should undoubtedly be taken

Interior of a long-house of the Trelleborg type. In the middle, the long, stone-paved fireplace. The smoke went out through a hole in the roof. The low benches along the sides were also used for sleeping.

Different types of Nordic houses. The upper three on the right had dug-down floors, and through this provided more room. In the top one, the walls consist of horizontal planks; the house below it is built of vertical staves; and the one below that, of a plait-work of withies daubed with clay. The second house from the bottom has turf walls, and the bottom picture shows an oblong house with clay-daubed walls and external oblique-posts that buttressed the roof. These larger houses had interior roof-bearing posts.

144

as only a protection round the house itself, which was built of wood. The saddle-roof was generally supported by two parallel rows of posts within the room. These were clearly in corresponding pairs, since they were attached at the top to cross-beams. Over those lay rafters and laths, which bore a roof-covering of straw or turf. Wood was therefore an indispensable material. For the outer walls weaker posts were used, mainly split or hewn tree-trunks. Several types of wall are known. The most common in Viking times seems to have been of wattle and daub. Where there were turf walls, vertical planks, 'staves,' were used as panels inside the turfs. But free-standing stave-houses with vertical planks, or log houses horizontally laid, also occur.

The clay walls had to have a foundation of wood. This consisted of split posts of the kind mentioned above, combined with a horizontal plait-work of withies. On to this firm core the clay was applied in a fairly thick layer, which was completely impervious. Two people had to work simultaneously at the daubing, one from each side.

During the Viking era, building with wood became more general. This is indeed taken for the most part to be a way of building typical of the Vikings, but in actual fact the method became common only in the Middle Ages. The horizontal logs are firmly slotted into each other at the ends. Remains of the packing between the logs have been found, especially in Finland. These fragments of clay have a characteristic triangular cross-section, with the impress of the two curved surfaces, which come to a point, and a more uneven third side.

The farmhouses themselves are thus fairly well known to us from excavations; but only ordinary buildings, none can be regarded as representing a royal manor.

In Norway, a typical settlement has recently been examined on a terrace in Årdalen, Sogn. Here had stood a group of houses surrounded by burial-mounds, but it is unlikely that all the houses were inhabited at the same time. A larger house had probably been in use, and in connection with it a pair of smaller ones. One of them measured only 4 × 7.5 metres internally. It was surrounded on three sides by thick embankments or walls of stone and earth, but the walls themselves were of wood. On the floor lay an open hearth, and in it was a hollowed-out roasting-pit, three-quarters of a metre in diameter, filled with fire-cracked stones. Such pits are well-known from the later prehistoric period, and they are also mentioned in the Icelandic Sagas. In order to roast, the stones were evidently heated in the fire and then packed down in the pit round the meat, fish, etc., which was protected from direct contact by a wrapping of green leaves or clay. It is an excellent way of roasting, which preserves the juices of the meat, and to judge by their general occurrence, these pits were much appreciated. On the other site were similar traces of a building.

Together the house layers have yielded a number of finds, on the one hand pieces of ornaments, and on the other implements and arrow-heads, as well as a bridle. So horses had been kept. Typical is the hand-mill, which had to be turned till the corn was finely ground. It was not surprising that this chore was assigned to the bond-women. A soapstone cauldron is native work, made in Norway, where they were hewn straight from the rock, and from where they were exported. It was a cheaper version of the metal cauldron, which was in fashion during the Viking period. One could cook soup, and much else, for the pot could be placed directly over the flames.

The sickle, scythe, and pick we shall come back to later (p. 157), as well as to some small implements which seem to have been used in the smithy. The arrow-heads were used both for fighting and for hunting. In Norway complete hunting equipment has been found many times in the mountain districts; arrow-heads, knives and spear-tips, necessary for hunters who procured their living in the wilderness. There was a demand for furs and skins.

In Sweden the foundations of many houses from the early iron age have been preserved, with strong stone-and-earth walls, particularly in Gotland and Öland. This type of house was largely replaced during the Viking period by buildings with wattle walls. Some interesting foundations have been examined at Levide in Gotland. The house was at least eighteen metres long and up to seven and a half metres wide, manifestly with curved sides. Quantities of clay daub have preserved the impress of the inner wooden structure of the walls. At one end there was a wall of wood. Many Swedish house-foundations from the same period might be mentioned. An interesting one is at Badelunda in Gotland, which is thought to have supported a boat-house. Corresponding discoveries have been made in western Norway and in Jutland. These foundations were oblong and seem to be particularly suitable for the protection of ships.

To these remains of wattle-and-daub houses may be added a couple of the foundations at Storhagen and some other sites on Åland. Storhagen had seven houses. The largest measures 10×22 metres, with the traces of post-holes for the roof and walls, as well as wide stone paving outside. Two of them—perhaps four—seem to have been timbered; they are quite small. One of the houses had a very simple structure, with the sloping roof resting directly on the ground. One gets an idea of the different functions of the buildings. Some of the houses were used as dwellings; others—without a hearth—were probably for stores, etc. The finds include ornaments, an iron key, loom-weights, a grind-stone, knives, a 'fire-steel' (to strike sparks, which were caught in tinder—the matches of the time) and shards of earthenware vessels. Part of a charred grain of wheat and some peas indicate agriculture and gardening.

This iron pot was once hung up on its long iron chain, ready to be filled with all that goes to make a decent meal. Right, a lamp with pointed stem, which was stuck into the floor. The hemispherical reservoir was filled with whale-oil, and a wick provided a modest light. The pot and the lamp from Oseberg are in the Viking Ship House at Bygdöy, Oslo.

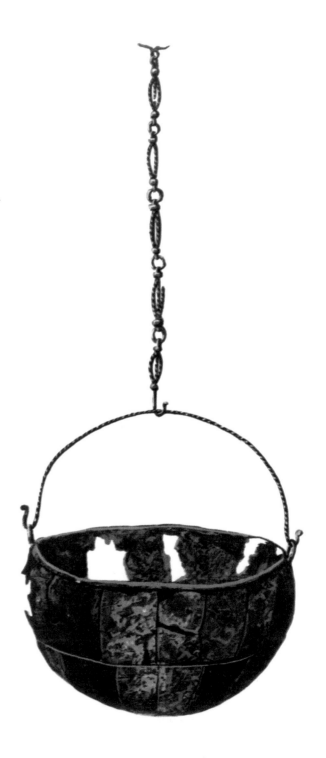

Interesting evidence on building conditions in Viking times in Denmark is given by Lindholm Höje, north of Ålborg, and by the remains of a village near the Viking camp at Aggersborg near Hobro, where two rows of houses have been found with slightly curved walls. At Lindholm Höje the buildings were from the later part of the period. Some had a rectangular plan, and some, like the foundations at Aggersborg, curving walls and post-holes outside, from slanting props to the wall-posts, a construction that is also found in Westphalia. There may well have been unpleasant experiences from the pressure of the great roof on the walls. Particularly noteworthy, however, is a complex of four long houses, built together, which constitute a forerunner of the modern farmhouse built round a yard. Besides open fireplaces, on the floors of the houses were ovens built of clay.

The space inside the house might be partitioned. In the actual living quarters there was a hearth in the middle of the floor which gave light and warmth. This might be oblong and paved, or merely a low elevation of clay. If peat was used, the smoke made one's eyes smart before one had even sat down. Here various occupations found a place: the weaving stood ready stretched, with its two posts, linked by a beam across the top on to which the material was gradually wound. The vertical threads were divided into two sets, which were held taut by weights below. These were mentioned above in connection with the Åland foundations. On the whole these round, pierced lumps of baked clay are among the most common finds at house sites. One of the sets of threads was swung forward, whereupon the yarn was passed through the shed between the stretched threads and beaten firm with the weaving 'spoon'. This might be of bone or iron, and is a frequently recurring element in burial-goods.

The raw material, wool or flax, could be worked at home. The flax was crushed with a wooden mallet—known from the Oseberg grave —in order to free the fibres. These were heckled with a tool related to that of later times, close-set with pins. The wool went through the same simple process that still goes on today. The simple construction of the wool-shears is the same as that still employed. Spinning was done with a distaff and a wooden rod called a spindle, which was furnished at the bottom, on its thicker part, with a whorl. This could spin evenly while the spinner formed the thread with light movements of the fingers. The stick on which the woollen thread was wound is also known, for example, in one from Oseberg. There, even a yarn-winder has been found, four horizontal arms on a stand, for the finished thread.

In the middle of the floor, the preparation of food might take place, if it was not still done outside in the open, or in another building. The low bunks along the walls provided places to sit, and at night they

A loom of the same type as that of the Viking era, and which was used right up to the last century in the Faeroe Islands. At the top it has a round bar from which hang the warp-threads, wound in bunches round weights, which hold the threads taut. One divided the warp-threads with a rod roughly in the middle of the loom, and then threw the shuttle with the weft-threads in between them. The weft was packed upwards with a comb or, as here, with a sword-shaped tool of bone. The finished material was wound round the bar at the top, while fresh warp-yarn was released from the hanging weights.

The scissors from the Århus find are of the same simple type as the sheep-shears that are still in use. The curved part provided tension and the sharp edges could cut cloth, wool and hair.

The spindle with its whorl of baked clay was an invaluable possession for an active woman. The carded ball of wool was wrapped round a stick, and after she had fastened a thread from the wool by a little hook at the top end of the spindle, she twisted the yarn by setting the spindle in rotation. Prehistoric Museum, Moesgård, Århus.

Below, a fragment of the very long-toothed comb that was used for packing the weft. Prehistoric Museum, Moesgård, Århus.

Wooden mallet of the type that was used for pounding the flax, to break down the stems.

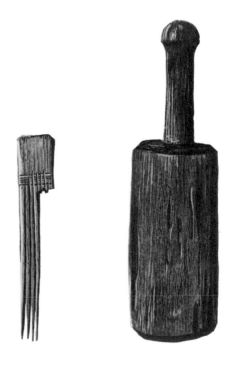

became places to sleep. It was still customary in many simple farm cabins to have animals at one end of the room.

On the floor in many houses, besides the open hearth, there was sometimes a roasting-pit or an oven. These ovens were made in the same way as the clay-covered walls, on a framework of wattle shaped like a beehive. The oven was heated up and the embers raked out, the bread was put in and one had not long to wait before one could open the access again and take out the small round loaves. The heat was effective, but the oven easily became brittle after being used for some time, and had to be repaired or rebuilt. The round pans of iron with long handles, which are found in many Norwegian Viking graves, were probably used for baking flat bread.

A common way of cooking food was to boil it in a suspended vessel. Apart from cauldrons of iron and bronze, very extensive use

was made of soapstone vessels, which were exported from the Norwegian quarries. At Oseberg a typical large iron cauldron with a handle has been found, roughly half a metre in diameter. It has a round bottom and must have hung the whole time by the handle, on a length of chain. When it was to go over the fire, it was hung from a tripod of iron, whose sturdy, twisted legs ended in sharp claws, so that they did not slip aside. The boiling of meat, soup and sausage was clearly customary, and we have fine proof in the saga account of the sacrificial feast at Tröndelag, where cauldrons boiled in the middle of the floor and Hakon Adelstensfoster had to bring himself to take part. Fatty vapours rose from the cauldron and settled on the handle in such quantities that one could taste them when one held one's mouth open over it, as Hakon was forced to do.

By the side of the fireplace stood oblong troughs and round scoops with short handles, carved in wood, dishes and bowls. At Oseberg both barrels and tubs were found whose staves were held together by bands. The tubs had handles. An iron axe and knives belonged to the necessary kitchen equipment of a larger household, and similarly, steel, flints and tinder had to be on hand in case the fire on the hearth went out.

Over the open fire, meat could be roasted on a spit. Both fork-shaped and single-pronged iron spits occur, and meat may well have been roasted also on the long-handled pans with flat, spiral-shaped ends, or in bread-pans.

The Oseberg farm, which was owned by a prominent family, had kitchen equipment that shows the needs of a large estate—at the least, it was not less than in the kitchen of a medieval castle: 3 iron cauldrons plus a tripod of the same material, 1 large and 3 small

Yarn-winder from the Oseberg grave. A reconstruction.

troughs, 5 scoops, 4 dishes and 7 bowls, 10 tubs and 1 barrel, all of wood, 2 axes, 5 knives and 1 millstone. But that was not all. We must reckon with still more implements of the above type, which for any reason were not preserved in the ship-burial. Many of the vats would in any case have been kept in store-rooms, insofar as they contained milk, meat (salted and smoked), etc.

Just as such a great man's establishment disposed of varying, and in part new-fashioned kitchen equipment, so too some of the house-hold goods show forms hitherto unknown in the north. First and foremost the beds, finely worked and made up with down bedding. Before this—and still among ordinary people—one man-aged with wooden benches round the walls. Beds took up much more space, and it is possible that they received a room of their own. There were no less than three beds in the Oseberg grave. The largest measures 2.2 × 1.9 metres at the bottom. The bed-posts at the head of the bed rise high and end in carved, bowed animal-heads. The other two beds are less substantial, but also well-made. Inside the bed-frame are horizontal cross-pieces on which some kind of mattress must have lain. The quilt itself was filled with bird's feathers. Similar quilts have been found in the rich Viking graves at Mammen, Jutland, amongst other places.

Two types of wooden chair are known, one of which is from Ose-berg. This is box-shaped, with a square back. The seat, which is 40 × 50 cms., was plaited of rope or bark. The height of the seat is

A banquet is being prepared and the cooks are zealously at work. The cauldron hangs over the fire, no doubt full of succulent meat soup. Further along, pieces of meat and birds on spits are waiting to be roasted over the fire. The baker takes the hot bread

gingerly out of the oven. On the right of the picture, preparations are being made for a serving. Bowls, knives and plates are laid out, and a man blows a fanfare. Detail from the Bayeux tapestry.

The kitchen equipment on a farm was extensive, not least when it came to the various forms of preserving-vessel, e.g. wooden bowls, tubs and barrels. In a large farm, like the one over which the distinguished Oseberg woman presided, accessories were used which were not inferior to those of the castle-kitchens of the Middle Ages.

The chair of the Oseberg woman, right, could be reconstructed on the basis of the considerable remains that were in the ship-grave. The chair is very low and has a plaited seat. The Viking Ship House, Bygdöy, Oslo.

38 cms., hence rather low. Finely executed chairs with back supports crowned with beautifully carved animal-heads, roughly like those on the great bed, have become known to us through Swedish finds and from the Bayeux tapestry. The other type of chair, which is known from Sweden, is the block-chair; it is round with a swung back, made from a thick tree-trunk.

No tables were found in the Oseberg grave, but through lucky circumstances the remains of one have been preserved in the Viking grave under Hörning church in east Jutland. The table can be reconstructed with certainty. It consists of a heavy frame of oak logs, which are slotted into each other and held together with wooden dowels. The table-top sits in the bottom of the frame, so that the table looks like a long box on four legs, 20 cms. high. Over all the

The largest and finest bed in the Oseberg grave was undoubtedly the distinguished lady's. Under a down quilt and on a comfortable mattress she will have slept well. One can only hope that the two enormous animal-heads shielded her from bad dreams. The inside length of the bed is only 1.65 m., while the width is 1.80 m. The three beds in the Oseberg find were unfortunately so poorly preserved that it was not possible to restore them. The ones now displayed at the Viking Ship House, Bygdöy, Oslo, are exact, full-size copies.

A domestic scene on a Gotland farm, as conceived by the artist of the picture-stone at Buttle, Änge. In the house, which is seen here in cross-section, sit two people on block-chairs of some kind in lively conversation, while a dog lies in the side part of the room.

table is only 30 cms. high and 50 cms. wide. This shows how low some of the furniture was—compared to this the beds seem almost high. On the Hörning table stood a bronze bowl, and the guess is that it was used for washing in. The sides of the table have beautiful chamfering, cut with a chamfering plane (see p. 62).

The well-to-do lady of the house was not content with the simple fabric that served for the making of everyday clothes. Like the Oseberg queen she had access to, for instance, the band-loom and the 'sprang'-loom (for a kind of knit-work), and to 'tablet-weaving.' The latter made use of small square pieces of wood with holes in each corner.

The housewife used a heavy, flattened lump of glass to smooth the material and the seams (like an iron), and as ironing-board she might have had a large plaque of whalebone with carved animal-heads. Such pieces are well-known finds from antiquity. The rich lady also needed a casket for her ornaments and wooden boxes for various small items, sewing things, combs, cups of wood and earthenware, etc.

A couple of truly noble caskets have been preserved in amazingly good condition right up to our time in the two German cathedrals of Bamberg and Cammin. The latter was unfortunately destroyed during the closing battles of the Second World War. Both have been highly esteemed and both have great interest for the history of art because of their perfect reliefs on the flat surfaces of walrus-ivory and elk-horn. We shall return to them in the chapter on art. It is

thought that the daughter of Canute the Great, Kunigunda, married to the Emperor Henry III, may have owned the Bamberg casket, and that the one in Cammin may have been identical with the casket which the Norwegian King Sigurd Jorsalafar gave to the Church of the Holy Cross in Kungahälla, and which was stolen by the Wends. These are hypotheses, but they are mentioned to emphasize how highly one must imagine such exceptional works of art were valued, and that they were not just made for the foremost women.

The Bamberg casket has a square ground plan with sides of 26.5 cms. and a height of 13 cms. The bronze edges that hold the flat surfaces together are finely decorated, and end in animal-heads. The Cammin casket was equally unique in its fine execution. It was no less than 63 cms. long, 33 cms. wide and 26 cms. high. The casket was in the form of a house, and played an important part in the reconstruction of such buildings as the Trelleborg houses. A panel in the upper part of the casket served as a lid. This could be locked with a key.

The farmhouses were surrounded by tilled fields and — especially in southern Scandinavia — by meadows. But it cannot be denied that conditions varied greatly. For northern Norway we have an authentic account, set down by King Alfred of England. It was told to him by an eminent man and sea-captain, Ottar. 'He had only 20 cows, 20 sheep, and 20 pigs. On the other hand, he owned riches which were more highly valued in his country, namely 600 tame deer which are called reindeer. The little he ploughed, he ploughed with horses.' His most important income came from the Finns in the form of tax: reindeer hides, birds' feathers (for quilts), whalebone and rope of whale or seal-skin (these were always praised as being extraordinarily strong). The leading Finns paid 15 marten skins, 3 reindeer hides, 1 bear-skin, 10 sacks of birds' feathers, 2 blouses, one of bear-skin and one of otter-skin, and two hide-ropes, each 60 ells long. Whaling was a major source of income up there, and Ottar related how he and five others had caught 60 whales in two days. Ottar maintains that these creatures could be up to 50 ells long. But the Norse sea-captain was probably not entirely devoid of imagination.

If one compares this picture of subsistence with conditions on Iceland and the Faeroes, one sees that time there was spent also in bird-catching, egg-collecting, gathering driftwood, searching for bog-iron, and tending flocks. Coming back, a study of the valleys and tilled fields of the southern part of Scandinavia, which is suited to agriculture, yields a different perspective, although there were opportunities for catching things even there. In each locality they had to adapt themselves to the prevailing conditions. For the energetic, there were chances everywhere, and the Norsemen searched vigilantly for areas they could exploit, quarries for bog-iron, soapstone and

This large casket, which up to 1945 was the most valuable piece in Cammin cathedral, was unfortunately destroyed at the end of the Second World War. It was a magnificent piece of work in elk-horn and gilded bronze, 63 cms. long. Fortunately we have casts and photographs of the casket; with its ornamentation in the Mammen style, it is one of the most notable examples of Scandinavian art. The town of Cammin now belongs to Poland and is called Kamień Pomorski.

schist for hones, etc. Each tract had its advantages and disadvantages. The forest was got rid of by setting it on fire, after a fire-trace had been cut. Burnt land provided room for livestock or for cultivation.

Agriculture, combined with stock-raising, remained the most common way of securing a living. Horses and oxen were used as draught animals. Their dung was spread on the fields. In the Oseberg grave a muck-rake has been found of the same characteristic form as has been used right up to the present day, a fork with a curved grip halfway down the shaft to hold on to with one hand. The dung was presumably carted out on a simple sledge of the type that has also been met with in the Oseberg finds. Sledges like this were used up to the 19th century in Norway, and it is typical that the sledge had

holes for lacing on the sides and ends. This corresponds to the arrangement found on later Norwegian dung-sledges, which had a kind of trough-shaped upper part lashed on with withies. While the grand sleighs were finely decorated with high cornerposts, the simple sledge clearly differed from them and must be regarded rather as a work-tool. Both the Edda poems and the older Frostating law mention manuring; the latter in detail, in that it says a fourth part of the land shall lie fallow and be manured. These sources undoubtedly reflect a tradition from Viking times.

It is evident from the written sources that muck-spreading and heavier digging work was carried out by the slaves. The spades were of wood. There were two sorts: one with a ledge for the foot, designed for breaking up the earth, the other with smooth shoulders like a shovel, and presumably used as such. There is a picture of workmen with the latter type of spade in the Bayeux tapestry; two of them are hitting at each other in jest. One notes that these spades are represented as having iron-shod edges, which does not occur in Nordic examples. Bearing in mind the many large earthworks of the Viking era—not merely those involved in agriculture—one must assume that this work was in general carried out by bondmen. According to the Icelandic Grágás code of laws, 'Grefleysingr,' i.e. free from fork or spade, is the designation for a freedman.

The earth was broken up with spade, hoe or a long pole with a broad iron tip, and especially with an *ard* plough or a mould-board plough. Small stony fields, particularly in the Scandinavian peninsula,

Although ice put a stop to sailing, it also opened up opportunities for journeys by other means. Ships were laid up and sledges and ice-runners brought out.

Ice-runners are far from rare in the early finds from the towns, but also in finds from dwellings in the country and in graves. A grave in Birka contained two ice-runners and an iron point that had obviously belonged on a pole. One stood bent forward on the carved pieces of bone, which were polished smooth on the under side, and poled oneself along. In this way, one could quickly reach the catching grounds, where one fished through a hole in the ice.

Fishing. In the boat sit two fishermen, one holding the rudder or an oar while the other spears a fish. Below is the outstretched net. Detail from a Gotland picture-stone from Ardre.

however, always required hand tools. Of the ploughs, many traces have been found in the form of iron shoeings for the coulter. They were presumably designed mostly for the pointed coulter, which makes a furrow, since coulters are always symmetrical, while a ploughshare is skewed. Right up to the present day, similar simple tools have been used, with drawing beam and guiding handles, and the tip pointing straight down, especially on loose earth. At all events, it could easily break up the surface of a reaped field. At Lindholm Höje the existence of a strange, and undoubtedly late type of arable field has been established with large parallel furrows, which make the crop stand in long, banked-up rows, reminiscent of asparagus beds. They stayed dry, since the water ran off in the furrows.

On heavier soils a mould-board plough was probably used, which could turn the earth. It is true we have no remains of ploughs of this type that can be clearly dated in the Viking period, but the plough was known considerably earlier on the Continent and in England, and traces have been established which can best be explained as plough-furrows nearer to a thousand years before the Viking period in the north. Furthermore, a typical wheel-plough is depicted on the Bayeux tapestry. On it one can also find a simple harrow, which was used before sowing. Simple wooden clubs or wooden hoes, found at Oseberg, seem to have had the same function as harrows. Or else they were used to bed down the seeds after sowing.

As draught animal Ottar mentions the horse, which must have sounded a trifle odd in England—on the Bayeux tapestry there are yoked oxen. We can certainly assume that oxen were used regularly, perhaps bullocks in particular, which were immensely strong, on heavy clay soils. But with the speedy horse one could do more. One could work larger fields, and hence get richer returns.

Another important means of increasing the yield has already been touched upon in connection with manuring. By letting an acreage lie fallow and giving it manure, one renewed the fertility of the soil. If in addition one could rotate between winter crop, spring crop and lying fallow, as was done in the Frankish kingdom, one made sure of a yield each year, even if some crops turned out poorly, and also obtained some larger harvests. Since the horse played an ever greater role as draught animal, it was important to have oats as an element in its fodder.

The crops we know not only from the carbonized remains of barley, rye, wheat and oats. In addition such vegetables as peas, onions and cress, etc., are mentioned in early sources   onions, not least, were very extensively cultivated for seasoning and fortifying purposes. The grain was cut with a sickle, which naturally took time, not least because crops grew so irregularly over the ground. As far

157

as we know there was no drainage other than the plough-furrows, and the height of the grain varied with damp and dry districts.

When the grain was cut, it had to dry. This probably occurred most often in the sheaf on the field, but in the Atlantic coastal areas there were presumably drying-houses. Then came threshing. Some clubs and sticks found in bogs have been taken to be threshing implements. So the grains of corn were laid out on a flat place and beaten. It is even possible that the flail was already known at that time. It was in use in central Europe several centuries earlier.

Before being ground, the grain had to be quite dry. Remarkably enough, proof has been found from the Iron Age that the grain was roasted beforehand. The kernels then split open more easily. That they then became mingled with stone-dust from the mill-stones may well have contributed to the fact that Viking people had more or less worn-down teeth. The powerful drying of the grain probably took place in a baking oven or on a stone slab by the hearth.

The domestic animals consisted of cattle, pigs, sheep and horses. In addition there were dogs and sometimes goats, which gave milk. In wooded districts in the south, pig-farming played a proportionately great part. The animals could be fed by sending them out to eat acorns and beech nuts. In the north, where there was dry, open pasture land, sheep-raising was particularly important. The sheep were of the primitive type with horns. All the domestic animals—except for some of the dogs—were decidedly small and very thin. The difficulty of procuring sufficient fodder for the winter undoubtedly affected the size of the animals. Butter and cheese are products that are often mentioned in the sources immediately after the Viking period. Sour milk of a different kind was certainly a common food in many places.

The horse and the dog were the favourites, and they sometimes followed their master into the grave. Grave-finds even include proper dog-collars and artistically finished straps with which a whole leash could be held in check. Some of the dogs—as the skeletons show—were powerful and had large, sharp teeth. Some were watch-dogs and others were used for hunting; some might well have been herd-dogs. Such fierce dogs were on the whole quite a help to the Vikings in defence.

Horses were used above all for riding. Many bridles and beautiful riding accessories have been preserved, and from Oseberg there is a finely carved wooden saddle. Several grave-finds of shoulder-bars, however, show that horses were often harnessed to a wagon. The animal was connected with a number of cultic ceremonies, and we have striking proof of this, as we shall see later.

The great problem for farmers at that time was to keep the domestic animals alive through the winter. In the far north, of course, this was

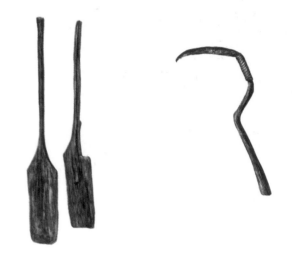

Agricultural work, as represented on the Bayeux tapestry.

One-sided and two-sided wooden spades have often been found in the vicinity of the great constructions of the Viking period, such as the Jelling mounds and the Danevirke, for example. The two spades on the left are from the Oseberg find.

The sickle was set on an extra, curved handle which made it easier to strike at the growing crop. From Hverven, Buskerud, Norway.

On light soils the *ard* was always used, a scratch-plough with iron point. Ploughs of the same type as the one shown below were used in Gotland and many other places in northern Europe right up to the present day. The plough illustrated is Polish, from the 11th century, and closely related to the implements of the Viking era.

especially difficult. There one had to reckon on keeping them indoors at least 200 days in the year, and since a cow needed roughly $12\frac{1}{2}$ kilos of hay per day, $2\frac{1}{2}$ tons would be necessary for each cow, 25 horse-loads, i.e. a horse had to struggle back from the meadow with its load 25 times to fetch enough to feed *one* cow through the winter. In addition to dried grass there was leaf-fodder, which was cut from the branches with a special knife, which was curved or had a hook at the tip to gather in the leaves.

Further south in Scandinavia it was not quite so hard, but demanding enough. In order to procure fodder for one cow a man had to work with his scythe for ten to sixteen days (depending a little on how accessibly the grass grew) to supply the winter's needs. For a herd of ten cows two men had to be haymaking and carting from early morning to late evening throughout a couple of months; and if in addition there were two horses, one had to reckon on extra work corresponding to the needs of four cows. Sheep, on the other hand, needed only a fraction of what the cows ate, roughly a sixth. Thus sixty sheep could be kept through the winter on the same quantity of fodder as ten cows or five horses. But to keep all these animals alive it was nonetheless necessary for six men to be fully occupied throughout the whole of the hay season.

In such circumstances we must reckon that procuring fodder took up a substantial part of the farm-workers' time. This is the reason why larger establishments either presupposed a large family—parents with children and their husbands, wives and children—or had a lot of bondmen or freedmen at their service. Working the land, sowing and reaping, hunting and fodder-gathering had to be done at the same time. This is why large farms must have had a considerable number of labourers; fifty to a hundred men could easily be occupied, when one also took on iron mining and building activities. The enterprising farmer had no need to let anyone's hands be idle.

At his side the farmer had his wife, who had just as much to do, producing the daily needs of food, ale and other drinks for the household, and preparing the winter stock of salted meat, etc. Even if she had helpers, the whole responsibility rested with her when the men

went off a-viking. It was not without reason that one such energetic housewife, Odindissa, received a memorial tribute from her surviving husband in these words, which can be truly appreciated only when one knows the background: 'There shall not come to Hassmyra a better house-mother who sees to the farm.'

She had also to look after the clothes and perhaps the footwear. It was not enough to spin and weave both coarse and fine materials; small accessories and decorative ribbons had to be cut out and sewn.

Outside, on the periphery of the farm, fire-hazardous and demanding work took place. Here trunks were hewn into planks and posts. With crude wedges trees were split apart. This occurred most easily with oak, which could be split radially, while there was a lot of waste in the shaping of most other types of tree, which gave only one or two planks from a trunk. Laboriously these were hewn out with a woodman's axe. There were adzes and straight axes, knives and chamfering planes, a simple little tool with a cross-piece with which one cut out chamfers on decorated edges. Added to which, in Viking times wood was one of the most valued materials for artistic activity. The wood-carvers were true masters at covering a surface with stylised and significant motifs, a sign of their intense delight in beauty, which received its finest expression in some of the possessions of the Oseberg queen.

At some distance from the dwelling-house there was also the smithy. It is probable that the actual smelting of the bog ore took place in the vicinity of the mine, if there was enough wood near by for making charcoal. The expert smiths knew the art of building a strong, chimney-like oven on a framework of wood with clay plastering. In it charcoal and ore were mixed, and under the influence

Above and below, parts of a beautiful set of riding equipment from the parish of Fors in Södermanland, Sweden. Stirrups reached the north from the south-east years before the Viking period and then became very common. Some forms bear clear traces of influence from the riding peoples of the east.

160

Above, detail from a picture-stone from Klinte, Hunninge, Gotland. It obviously concerns a fight at the entrance to an enclosure with houses. An ox stands tied up on one side and men shoot arrows at each other.

Although the roads at that time were not good, one could get along by horse and wagon, picture far left. The body of the wagon rested on a fork-shaped chassis to which the axles were attached, see p. 193. Detail from the representation on the Gotland picture-stone from Alskog.

of a carefully estimated amount of heat the ore was made to take up just as much charcoal as was needed, and to be separated out as a spongy mass, which was then worked with a hammer.

The work that followed was carried out in the smithy. Here were hammer and tongs, anvil and water trough, and the forge with its two bellows, which pressed out air through a clay pipe on to the charcoal and made it give off a powerful heat. So that he should not be exposed to this, the bellows-treader and his appliance were protected by a semi-circular stone, often ornamented, with a hole for the air-supply through the pipe. The smith could work the iron on the anvil, hammer it into the right shape, and weld two pieces together so that the join could hardly be seen. Swords were made in a masterly manner by welding two hard edges on to a softer central part. This central part was sometimes welded together out of iron-matter of varying hardness, which gave it an artistic, patterned finish. Behind many of the apparently simple tools and weapons lay a brilliant technique, which was unique in the world of that time. The Vikings were well aware of the importance of having the best weapons. It is understandable that they followed the destinies of famous swords and remembered the exploits in which they had a part. The eminent smith was a man to admire, and the legend of the master-smith Volund was related during the whole of the Viking period.

Town Life

Trade had long been important to the economy of the north, where many areas suffered from a lack of important raw products, but at the beginning of the Viking era it received a definite upsurge. There was a greater demand not only for luxury goods but also for metals, salt and other necessaries. In return, such goods could be exported as furs, hide ropes, slaves (some were war-booty), animals and agricultural products. What had previously been on a modest scale now received thorough treatment. This source of income changed people's way of life. Markets and imports grew and became regular. Where there was a good opportunity to introduce iron, for example, production went up considerably. Specialization was the best solution, both in the case of introducing earthenware, which was now turned as a regular craft, and metalwork.

While coins had previously been used only occasionally, there now came from the east, with the beginning of the Viking era, a heavy flow of silver coins, which stimulated turnover. Separate coins were of no interest to the Norsemen; they wanted reliable metal and safeguarded themselves with fine weight and touchstone. Even if the stamp on a foreign coin appeared to guarantee its worth, the Norse merchant was still sceptical at first and used coins in the same way as metal bars: when necessary he broke them into smaller pieces in order to obtain the agreed amount.

That connections between the north and its trading partners were really excellent appears from the rich finds of treasure—some with thousands of coins—which reveal that the trade was profitable. Clearly, a new situation had arisen in the north.

For both merchants and craftsmen the town became the natural setting for all their activities. Here the enterprising settled in just as they did on the Continent and in England. The town gave protection to the lone individual and the freedman. Here a new form of association was created in the guilds. Those who had been kept under in the country by the clannishness of the families could now make themselves felt.

On the lower reaches of the Rhine lay Dorestad, whose short, rich life was cut off abruptly in about 850. Along the whole of the North Sea coast towns sprang into existence. They usually consisted of a long street of close-packed houses which led to a harbour. On the Elbe there was Hamburg, and futher east, the town of Reric. Along the southern Baltic coast towns grew up at suitable places for transshipment or for markets: Wollin in the mouth of the Oder, Truso at

Large earthenware jar found at Slite, Gotland, 49.5 cms. high. It was doubtless used for preserving food, perhaps honey. During the Viking era earthenware vessels were still modelled and built up on a slowly-rotating wheel. It was only later that the rapidly-rotating potter's wheel came into use and made it possible to draw up an earthenware vessel from a lump of clay.

the outflow of the Vistula, and further north, Wiskianten and Grobin, with colonies from Gotland and central Sweden. On the Russian rivers towns grew up as in central and western Europe. And the transverse trade routes also gained in importance. From Prague one could go eastwards via Cracow to Kiev. From Staraya Ladoga and —later—Novgorod in northern Russia one could follow the natural paths to Kiev and further south to the Black Sea. The merchants knew and sought out these growing, trade-hungry towns. Although their population was predominantly heathen, for reasons of common sense a certain tolerance often prevailed. Respect was shown towards rich strangers with other religious views, and their priests were allowed to function.

The same applied also to the Nordic towns, which gained in importance during this period of growth. Hedeby lay on the best connecting route across South Jutland. Birka lay sheltered in Lake Mälar, and yet was easily accessible. Ribe faced the south-west, and Århus the east and north, and formed a connection with Kaupang on the coast of southern Norway.

Board-games were very popular during the Viking period. Several are known, such as this one, which comes from the excavations at Tyskebryggen in Bergen. It may be, at the earliest, from the end of the Viking era. It is not known exactly how many pieces were used, but there were evidently two different sets, one with white pieces and the other with coloured or black ones. One such game was *hnefatafl,* which is known from early Icelandic sources. It was played on a board marked in squares, with 12 bone or glass pieces against 13. Among the dark pieces was a king-piece, *hnefi*. The moves were made by throwing dice, several of which have been found.

The oldest are Hedeby and Birka, which were well-known to Christian missionaries. Both had a strangely limited life-span. They were rapidly developed, only to lose their importance all at once and be abandoned.

We first hear of Hedeby in 804, when the town is mentioned in the Frankish annals as Sliestorp, on the border between Denmark and Saxony. King Godfred's fleet and cavalry were assembled here. The town was clearly a starting-point for attacks against Charlemagne's northward expansion. Four years later, mention is made of a wall from sea to sea, with only one opening for horses and wagons. This refers quite obviously to one of the embankments of the Danevirke. It opened for the traditional route, which passed through. Along this, right down to our own times, people had conveyed goods or driven herds of oxen, horses, sheep, geese and other merchandise that could make its own way. It may be imagined that here, as at so many other places, the ruler of the land saw the advantage of levying toll on the thoroughfare.

For this year, 808, we have an important piece of information about Slesvig-Sliestorp-Hedeby (undoubtedly several names for the same town). King Godfred devastated Reric, which had brought his kingdom great gains through taxes. He carried off the merchants, weighed anchor, and arrived with the whole of his army at the harbour called Sliestorp. Here he evidently forced the merchants from Reric to settle. They now found themselves under his direct control and gave him the income he had enjoyed before.

Income from the towns was clearly something the ruler could count on, partly in the form of duties and market fees, partly in fines and direct taxation (for every hearth); the latter is mentioned in the oldest town regulations from Slesvig, to which the inhabitants of Hedeby evidently removed during the latter part of the 11th century. The towns therefore provided the ruler with an important income, and he must have been quite anxious for more of them to be established. His other opportunities for income were limited, and it is understandable that he had a permanent representative, a bailiff *(ombudsman)*, on the spot who looked after his interests, and who probably also took part in the town Thing. He may also have organized the defences and arranged for help from the ruler in the event of attack.

We know Hedeby from excavations, which have shown that, up to the Viking era, there were originally three villages spread along the Baltic Sea bay of Schlei (Sli). At the beginning of the actual Viking era, the settlement was concentrated at the mouth of a river that runs out into the bay, and this nucleus was slowly enlarged, so that during the first half of the 10th century it was surrounded by a great semi-circular embankment, 10 metres high, which enclosed an area of 24 hectares. The river silted up, and on the canal that was formed the houses lay close together. Gradually the whole area became covered with houses. The western edge had previously been a cemetery. A harbour was constructed with curved breakwaters that gave protection to the ships, which could lie at anchor here. The surrounding area was left open, as the Nordic name indicates (hede = heath). The open stretches may have been covered with heather. Clearly interest in the place lay in its excellent position as a trading centre, and nothing was expected from the fertility of the soil.

That it was a permanent settlement, and not merely temporary market booths, is shown by the well-constructed buildings. Besides dug-out houses, which belonged to the earliest period, and the settlement on the periphery, there were in the nucleus-area around the river larger and smaller houses of from 3×4 metres to $6\frac{1}{2} \times 15$ metres. Several types are found side by side, surrounded by small fences. The ground plan is rectangular, and the roof saddle-shaped. Some had wattle walls on vertical posts and internal roof-bearing posts. The walls of these were plastered with clay. Others were constructed of timber, thick horizontal planks between vertical posts. Yet others had 'stave' walls. It was a rich variety of building-methods, which is natural when so many different people come together.

The semi-circular embankment is part of the great system of earthworks which is known as the Danevirke, and which consisted of several lines of defence. The main embankment, which covers the raised trunk of Jutland from east to west, is linked by a rampart with the Hedeby embankment. A little further south and almost parallel runs the Kovirke ('cow work'), an older or contemporary defence-

Diagrammatic view of the extent of the Danevirke, from the Baltic Sea, and the semi-circular rampart round Hedeby, to Hollingsted, up to which the water-courses from the North Sea, the Eider and the Treene, were navigable. The defence-works run across Jutland, with an opening for the ox-route, the traditional route which runs in a north-south direction through the peninsula. The straight embankment in the southeast is called the Kovirke ('cow work'), and the powerful fortifications north-west of it are the main embankment itself. This was particularly strong and was reinforced during the Middle Ages by King Waldemar.

A reconstruction of that part of Hedeby which has been excavated by Professor Herbert Jankuhn. We see a bit of the town round the river, with its revetted banks. The houses were sometimes enclosed by low wooden fences and the roads were paved with wood.

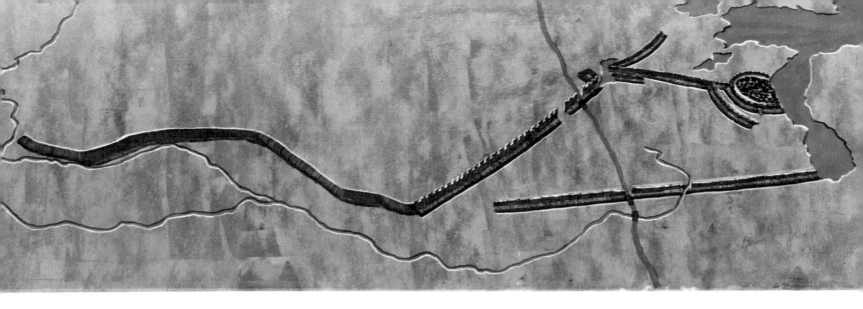

To obtain iron from bog-ore during the iron age and the Viking era, one used furnaces of the type reconstructed here. Similar furnaces have been used in Nigeria right up to the present day. In the top of the furnace was a mixture of charcoal and bog-ore in a ratio of 1:10. The temperature in this part of the furnace might amount to 1,400°C. Lower down the slag was smelted out and strained off into the bottom of the pit through a filter of straw. The iron was left hanging in lumps in the innermost part of the furnace, which stood about 1.5 m. high above the ground.

work. Both allowed the traditional route to pass, but provided the possibility of control and of ensuring that at all events plunderers who got through would have difficulty in returning with much booty. Further west, the embankment continued towards Hollingsted, which acted as a harbour for the river Treene and could be reached by boat from the North Sea. The Danevirke thus protected also a route from west to east.

As a cosmopolitan trading town Hedeby was visited by large numbers of foreigners. They looked with wonder on this strange community and returned home with some remarkable tales. At-Tartushi, for example, the Arab traveller, describes the inhabitants as worshippers of Sirius, apart from a few Christians who had their own church. Animal sacrifices were hung on poles in the courtyards, but for the most part the town was poor; babies could be put to death. Women had the right to divorce. 'Never have I heard more atrocious singing than that of the people of Slesvig; it is a growling which comes from the throat and sounds like the howling of a dog, only even more like a wild beast.'

We shall come back later to the value of such observations of a slightly fanciful nature. More important without doubt are the direct accounts from the first missionary period. Hedeby was the natural starting-point, for well-off Christians came there who were of benefit to the town and must have enjoyed the King's protection. One quite simply could not allow people whose presence was a prerequisite for the development of the town to be treated as having no legal rights. This appears from the *Life of St. Ansgar* (Chapter 24): 'In Sliaswich, a harbour in his (the Danish King Horik's) kingdom, very suitable for this purpose, where merchants converge from all quarters, he allowed him to erect a church, and he put a house at his disposal

167

where the priest could live. Similarly he allowed everyone in his land to become Christian if he so wished . . . For there were already many Christians there who had been baptized either in Dorestad or in Hamburg, and some of these were even reckoned among the notables of the town . . . Many were converted, so that also men from this people, without fear, and merchants both from here and from Dorestad, gladly sought out the place—which earlier they had not dared— and on this occasion prosperity prevailed throughout the town.' These events in the early 9th century were seen from the viewpoint of Hamburg. It was also from this Continental church that Ansgar's successor Rimbert (who was Archbishop of Bremen from 865—88) was sent on dangerous missionary journeys to the north. On one of these he came to Hedeby, from where he gave a vivid account of his experiences and of the gloomy atmosphere that prevailed in the age of slave-hunting. The Christians lived in anguish and had difficulty in redeeming their fellow-believers who had been carried off or bought by enterprising Vikings. In point of fact, the trade in human beings was undoubtedly one of the most important sources of income. There was a demand, namely, both from the east and from the south. Rimbert relates:

'Once when he (Rimbert) came to the land of the Danes, where he had built a church for the new Christianity at a place called Sliaswich, he saw a lot of Christians being led away in chains. To be seen among them was a nun, who, as soon as she caught sight of him in the distance, by falling on her knees and perpetually bowing her head, wished as much to honour him as to awaken his charity, so that she might be given her freedom. And so that he should understand that she was a Christian, she raised her voice and began to sing psalms. The Bishop was moved with compassion, and in tears he prayed to God that He might help her. At his prayers, the chain that held her bound was at once broken from her neck. Yet she was unable to escape, as the heathens soon reached her and caught her. Then the holy Bishop was moved with anguish and compassion for her, and while the heathens held her fast he began to offer all sorts of gifts for her. But they would agree to nothing less than that he should give them his horse, which he had for his private use. Nor did he refuse to do this, but jumped at once from the horse, and gave it with all its equipment in exchange for the slave-girl. And when he had redeemed her, he gave her her freedom and let her go where she wished.'

In such ways, glimpses have been preserved of the history of Hedeby during this upsurge under Danish sovereignty, the brief Swedish dominion at the beginning of the 10th century, and then the conquest by the German King Henry in 934. After that, it came back under Danish rule.

Slesvig, a -*vig* name, is Old Saxon or Old Frisian, as was already

Through the middle of Jutland, from Viborg southwards to the Elbe, runs the ox-route. Along the many parallel wheel-tracks, which here and there cut deep into the sand, one can see burial-mounds. These would be seen by wayfarers and in this way the deceased attained a sort of life hereafter, recalled and commented upon with a word of remembrance. Not only oxen, though these were undoubtedly the most common along the route, but also many other kinds of animal were driven south to be bartered or converted into silver coins.

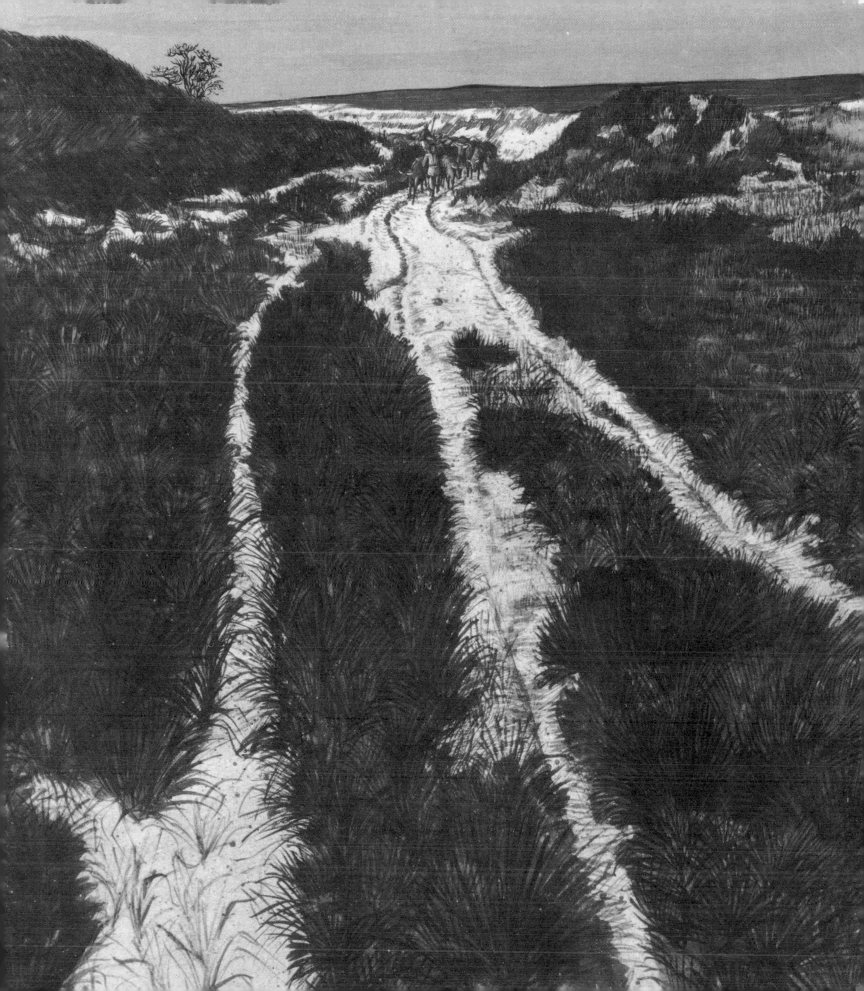

stated by a contemporary Anglo-Saxon, while the Danes said Hedeby. Later the name Slesvig was obviously attached to the present town further north, which succeeded Hedeby as the chief place in the area.

Hedeby was abandoned in the 11th century. The latest coin found in the town is from the time of Edward the Confessor (1042—1066). A poem has been preserved about one of the disastrous events during its last days, the attack by Harald Hardrade in 1049. It helped to give Hedeby the *coup de grâce*.

> From end to end
> Hedeby we burned.
> A mighty deed we did,
> This surely all must grant.
> To Sven we gave good cause
> To grieve. By night near dawn
> I saw the town in flames,
> High from the houses raging.

The other early Viking town was Birka, situated on a little island in Lake Mälar, easy to reach from the sea, and close to the route of those coming from the south who crossed the water to get to Uppsala. Birka too was surrounded in the 10th century by a semi-circular embankment, which had a series of characteristic openings. These were presumably where wooden defence towers had stood. The

Birka, as one might imagine it looked when one approached by boat. On the right are the defence-works of the hill-fort, to which the inhabitants could withdraw in the event of more severe attacks on the town. Just below the hill are the quarters for the town's garrison. The town itself was surrounded on the land-side by a semi-circular defence-wall, which was probably completed on the lake-side by pile-works in the water.

These ornaments, a necklace and a bracelet from a grave in Birka, provide a good picture of the motley connections of the trading town. Mixed together here with amber and objects such as the little rectangular piece with animal-decoration of typical English-Rhineland origin, are glass beads and bronze fragments from the Orient. State Historical Museum, Stockholm.

170

embankment undoubtedly had a wooden palissade at the top and a steep exterior reinforced with wood. It needed to be more effective than a pure earth embankment. Within the wall the houses must have stood right next door to each other. At least two types have been found, one with wattle-and-daub walls which we recognize from Hedeby, the other with thick timber walls in which the spaces were stopped with clay and moss. Preserved pieces of this packing material which have been found, with triangular cross-section, show the construction. Although nothing remains but a massive culture layer, ploughed through and spoiled, 'black earth,' there is sufficient proof of settlement, which came, however, just like Hedeby many years later, to an abrupt end. Already at the close of the 10th century, when the oriental trade and the stream of silver from the east dried up, Birka's fate was sealed.

But until then, the prevailing atmosphere had something of what we associate with the Wild West. On the south side lay the hill, 30 metres high, whose wall offered refuge during an attack. To the south and east stretched the largest known burial ground from this period, 3,000 graves with varied, sometimes rich equipment, which tells us better than anything else about the life and interests of the inhabitants, their ornaments and weapons, rare foreign objects and domestic miniatures in metal. There is a striking amount of evidence to be found of winter journeys: ice-spikes, skates and sledge runners of bone, etc. The great days for Birka were those when the fur hunters arrived with a good catch. They reached the town on skis and sledges;

when ice covered the lakes and bays it was easier to travel than in the summer. When the ice broke up and disappeared, the ships came back and steered for the natural harbours by the town. Here they could lie to with ease.

Not far from Birka lay Adelsö, where there was probably a royal demesne during Birka's heyday. Although Birka had a bailiff appointed by the King, its inhabitants were quite independent. They held their own Thing, but had to pay tax to the King.

A Norwegian counterpart was Kaupang in Skiringssal. The name is found at other places along the Norwegian coast, and indicates a trading locality. But in Skiringssal the place had a special importance, which is clear from the fact that it is mentioned by King Alfred through the account of the Norwegian sea-captain Ottar. From the town sailing routes ran to the west and south, amongst other directions. The numerous graves in the vicinity have preserved quite a number of objects that are Anglo-Saxon, Scottish or Irish, which underlines the contact with the west.

The other route, from central Scandinavia to Jutland and Hedeby, had lively use, as we can see from scattered finds on the east coast of Jutland, of Norwegian soapstone vessels, for instance, or axe-blades on their own, twelve collected on one haft, presumably from wrecked ships. Some fragments of soapstone have been found in Limfjord, and a concentration of them in the Viking town of Aros, the town at the river-mouth, boldly founded out on the Kattegatt. To it came ships from the north, east and south. It was a natural export harbour, situated just where the land-route along the east coast crossed the river. Three metres below the present centre of Århus, on a small gravel island surrounded by beach and low-lying land, are the remains of the town. An embankment from the 10th century was its protection and in the bend of the river ships could find lee—if they came on a peaceful errand.

Attacks, that is to say, were the inevitable consequence of enterprise and prosperity. Without defence-works and a powerful protector, it is inconceivable that ordinary people would have consented to live crowded together in a mass out there. Århus, like other early towns, was on crown land, i.e. it was founded on land that according to the earliest sources (which are later, however, than the foundations) belonged to the King. He either made it available for the purpose without losing his ownership, or else he acquired land with the intention of founding a town. We perceive an organizing will and a plan. Only the King can have possessed the means of power and the interest for such town building.

The place was suitable as a trading station, and to a certain degree for craftsmen, but not for anything else. It cannot have been pleasant out on the gravel islet, especially when the water-level rose in the

An armed Viking on horseback. This well-made little figure in silver was found in a grave at Birka. Ca. 2.7 cms. high. State Historical Museum, Stockholm.

Top left, a heavy iron key from the Viking town of Århus. Below it, two hunting arrow-heads. The lance-shaped arrow-head of iron, bottom, was found with other similar ones at the same place. In a rain of danger they once swished down upon the town. Above left, the Viking's matches, the 'fire-steel' with which he struck fire on flints. The sparks were caught in tinder and blown into flames. The fish-hook is also a find from the Viking town of Århus. Prehistoric Museum, Moesgård, Århus.

The iron forms for axes were exported twelve at a time. This appears from ancient sources but also clearly from this find, which was made at Gjerrild Strand, near Grenå on the east coast of Jutland. The axe-forms are threaded on to a stick of Norwegian spruce, which at that time did not grow in Denmark. Presumably they were from a sunken merchant ship. They came from northern Scandinavia and were perhaps intended for the town of Århus, which lay a little to the south of the place of discovery. The stick is 73 cms. long. National Museum, Copenhagen.

sea and the river. The damp sometimes oozed into the dug-out houses. But the freer living conditions, the security behind the wall and the good trade were sufficient compensation for the discomfort. It was a place for specialists. Behind lay the hilly landscape with the farmers' fields and buildings. Not far away to the north-west was the seat of a prosperous family, where the wife wore a pair of the most beautiful oval adornments that we have from the early Viking period. It was hardly people from these farms who felt like moving out on to the islet.

All the same, there were connections between the farms and the town. The latter could not get along without necessaries and thus acted as a stimulus to the farmers. In the town they could find an outlet for foodstuffs. For the very reason that the townspeople were specialists, like the warriors, they had to procure a great deal of what they needed from others. They had the means to buy goods, and this gave an impetus to the production of many energetic farmers. Only during the years after the Viking period, when trade declined, did the town-dwellers begin to support themselves with animals and take to the soil in gardens and small holdings.

One area of the town has been examined, the wall with the wood-covered path inside and the houses nearest to it. The men fit to bear arms could turn out quickly and man the exposed places on the wall, by running on to this ring-way. That attacks did occur we can see from the many arrow-heads that have been found embedded in the wall. Right under the foundations of a burned-down house, more-over, lay a skeleton without a head, who by all appearances was a victim of war, since the man was not buried, although there was a burial ground outside the town. He was merely thrown down with some of the debris from the destruction, an unknown, forgotten man.

The houses on the edge of the town were simple and astonishingly small. They are dug out a little, so that the saddle roof rested directly on the surface of the ground or only a little above it. Under a slight projection, one went down a few steps and then stood in the room with two low wall-benches set at an angle in a corner. In the middle might be the hearth, and by the wall a loom or other work tools. It was the abode of the common man in the town, one would have thought in fact of the poor, perhaps next to the slaves. Here there was only room to sleep and work. That the houses were nevertheless not so poor is shown by the ornaments and useful everyday articles such as combs, distaff weights, flax hackles, spurs, etc. On one of the combs there is even a name, Haegwin. If we had found these things as grave-goods, we should have considered the owner to be well-off.

Further into the town was undoubtedly where the richest chose to live. Here a beautiful mount from a drinking horn was found, with a frieze of birds which testifies to the artistic quality of the craftsmanship. The same applies to the decoration on the grave-stones from Århus, which manifestly come from a burial ground right outside the town wall. A stone decorated with a mask is one of the most effective works of art from the late Viking period.

These grave-stones take us into the environment in a different way from the excavations. Here the inhabitants step forward, with their names and their destinies. Just as the comb with the name in runes gave a glimmer of light in the murky, semi-subterranean room, and allowed a glimpse of one of its inhabitants or one of his friends, so do six grave-stones from Århus tell us in a stirring way of the life of the town. The period speaks through their names, a mixture of familiar and odd-sounding words like Käld, Ful, Inge, Rolf, Åmunde, Ögot, Gunulv and Asser Saxe. The last-named is called 'the greatest non-villain among men,' which for those days was praise indeed, even if it merely freed him from the burden of guilt. That he was wealthy appears from the fact that he owned a ship, with another man called Arne. This is a kind of partnership which we hear about several times, also in the running of a farm. It was natural that men should get together when it was a matter of procuring such a valuable adjunct as a trading vessel; both the gains as well as the risks were then shared. What is remarkable is that this partnership was evidently purely businesslike—unless Arne was already dead—for he took no part in the erection of the memorial stone. This was done, on the contrary, by his comrades Torste, Hove and Tvebjörn, who may have been sea captains or perhaps close friends. As we have seen, 'comrade' indicates the affinity which warriors, for instance, might have for each other. This Asser Saxe is in fact represented as being very well off. He belonged to the aristocracy of the town or the district.

The Viking town of Aros, remains of which have been found in the present Århus. The town's present harbour is situated outside the original coastline as seen here. The town, seen from the north, is surrounded by a wall. Outside were marshes, which helped to make it difficult of access. The town was open towards the sea, as far as one can judge. Only a little bit of the oldest part has been examined as yet, but we know that it played a large part as harbour for traffic to the east and north. In the drawn reconstruction, the church to the west of the wall was not yet built; it was erected in the middle of the 11th century.

Ful's impressive memorial stone with mask, which was supposed to ward off evil and strike terror. On its three sides one may read: 'Gunulv and Ögot and Aslak and Rolf raised this stone after their comrade Ful. He found death . . . where kings fought.' The stone was found at Århus, so the daring Ful was probably a man from the Viking town, and was buried immediately outside the burial ground. Prehistoric Museum, Moesgård, Århus. 1.6 m. high.

That there was contact with Hedeby is borne out by another stone; but apart from this name, only a small part of the inscription is preserved. It may be that the man had died there. The above-mentioned Ful, who had a particularly effective mask-stone raised over him, received a magnificent tribute: 'He found death where kings fought'—a well-found expression for a great Viking battle, undoubtedly at sea.

If, to these great men from the distinguished houses of the town, we add their women and children, the ordinary townspeople, the freedmen and slaves, foreign merchants, priests, monks and nuns, and such specialists as the master of the mint and the artist-craftsman, we begin to feel the atmosphere. The view from the town over the open sea was a broad horizon, which was sometimes broken by a sail. Then everyone gathered on the beach to see whether it was people they knew, or whether they could expect a visit bringing misfortune. They noted the way the ship was handled and manoeuvred. In this there was always something that could be recognized, and if it was friends and welcome sea captains, they were helped in and had the gang-board laid out. It was always exciting to hear news from strange and unknown lands; and who did not want to see what the ship had brought and hear what was wanted in exchange? In groups the new arrivals and the residents strolled together on the plank-covered way past dwellings and workshops, where operations were in full swing. Outside one of the houses lay a pile of deer-horn and bone that had been sawn into pieces for carvings and for combs, which lay on the floor, finely worked. In another place, round mill-

175

A reconstructed section from the part of Viking Århus which has become known through recent excavations. Along the inside of the wall runs a roadway paved with wood, which was also of importance in the defence of the town. A little way in from the roadway are the groups of houses, most of them very low, so-called pit-houses, small, square buildings with floors sunk into the earth.

One such house is shown below in cross-section. From ground level one went down into the house through a little porch with a few steps. It had obviously been a weaving-house; found in the little room was an upright loom. Low benches and a small fireplace made life more tolerable for the weaver.

Material and partly-worked piece for e.g. combs. Horn ornaments were fashioned with a short, sharp iron saw. Cp. p. 62.

The bone comb is made out of several pieces joined together. It bears the name Haekwin in the runic inscription, which was presumably the name of the owner of the comb. The Viking-town, Århus.

The flute, which is carved from bone, has a familiar shape. Similar instruments have been played right up to the present day. But it would certainly be interesting to know how the melodies sounded in the Viking era. Prehistoric Museum, Moesgård, Århus.

stones of dark basalt might be seen, which had been imported from the Rhine valley, and piles of leather for shoes. The craftsman in bronze was busy in his workshop on the decoration of sheet metal. The smith was working in a similar great din. His anvil rang with hammer-blows. Made here were arrow-heads, swords, spear-tips and axes. But softer tones might also be heard. Somewhere a flute was being played. One went by the master of the mint, who was beating his stamp into the sheet silver and laying out Århus coins one beside the other. Life and movement, both indoors and out. But space was cramped, and one soon came up against the wall that rose around the whole human throng. Roads led out through the town gates. One ran to the west, past the church, right outside the town. It stood high, with its grey limestone walls, an impressive feat of building. In the summer one could find coolness in there, and admire the crypt with its forest of square pillars. Here the bishop and clergy had their place, and from here special ceremonies went forth to gladden the Christians, not least strangers from the south and from the west who professed this faith. The bronze-worker inside the town had his best customers here. The church gave commissions which he had to exert himself to carry out well.

The town lay notably strange and exciting in the peaceful landscape. Outside lived the farmers. They followed the simple rhythm of nature and the seasons. Within the walls another way of life prevailed, and continual agitation. The families still made themselves felt, and the king was in the background, but it was the new and energetic men who got to the top, not only the well-born. Here there were opportunities for the bold, and in distinction to the Viking expeditions, often of a more lasting nature. The town became one of the instances of the dynamic in the period. It helped to transform the existence of the peoples of the north.

The Thing

One might perhaps wonder that law and order were able to make themselves felt during the Viking period. But people's sense of justice had a constant influence on their conduct, and called forth a reaction when it was violated. They accepted a pattern of life which took into consideration a man's honour and his demand for retribution. Christianity had not yet set any decisive stamp on society, and the concept of peace was not something unconditionally good. They might wish each other a good year; but who knew whether peace was always for the family's good.

At any rate, one could not stand idle in the face of attack and murder, for it was the concern of the whole family. Everyone answered for the actions of his kinsmen. The responsibility was distributed between two groups, according to kinship on the father's side and the mother's. We have already seen how death affected the succession, first in the father's family and then in the mother's (see p. 138).

If one man was killed by another, the whole of the killer's family were guilty of the crime and were threatened with revenge from the killed man's family. Blood revenge would be the consequence if they did not settle for a fine, which was determined according to an ingenious, well-thought-out system. If this did not work, it might be more honourable for the injured family to kill the foremost man in the murderer's family than the killer himself. The receiving of the fine was also a matter for the family, and although it was the killer who in the first place was answerable for paying the fine, his relatives might also risk being exiled if the money was not paid out.

In the same way, relatives—and friends—had to come forward to guarantee a person's truthfulness. Unity was so fundamental that relatives made no bones about taking over fatherless children. The sense of justice paid great regard to the family, therefore, as the proper foundation of society.

If a man belonged to a great family his influence might be extended, especially at the Thing. It was here that the sense of justice was formed and found expression. With the rise of the towns, not only the farmers (from a hundred), but also the town-dwellers (from a *birk*) had a place where they could meet and decide legal matters. Above these local Things stood the provincial Thing, which sometimes had to arrive at the final decision. Each province had its own legal usage, and its justice was valid therefore only within it. Banishment meant a ban on returning to one such province, which consisted, for example, of an area such as Skåne. Ansgar had already come

178   Thingvalla. Caption on next page.

across the importance of the Thing. The King let first Birka's Thing, and then the higher Thing decide whether Christianity might be preached in the Swedish town. The Thing was independent of the King as a court of law and source of legislation. When it came to it, the King had the same right to vote as any one else who took part. He could put forward suggestions, and his influence might be great and his powers of persuasion considerable, but it could also happen that the men of the Thing went against him; even the making of foreign policy was sometimes discussed by a provincial Thing. The atmosphere, as one can understand, easily became heated during such discussions. Through Snorre we have a reliable account—as it seems—of the Thing-meeting at which Olof Skötkonung and Torgny the Law-man exchanged words. One can readily imagine the scene, the open place with the little circle of trusty men sitting on beams laid across the Thing-stones. Outside stood the men of the Thing, free farmers, self-conscious and ready, by a murmur or a clatter, to make known whether they were for or against the speaker. Thus spoke Torgny: 'Torgny, my grandfather, remembered King Erik Emundsson and said of him, that all the time he was in his most agile years he raised levies and went off to other lands, and placed under him Finland and Karelia, Estonia and Kurland and many countries in the east, and one can still see the earth forts and other great works he carried out . . . I can still remember Erik the Victory-happy, and I was with him on many forays; he increased the kingdom of the Swedes and defended it bravely.' Torgny was opposing Olof Skötkonung's plan to go west to Norway and wanted him to be reconciled with Olav the Thick and marry his daughter Ingegerd. Torgny wanted the expedition to go east again, and promised that, 'If you will win back to yourself the kingdoms in the east which your kinsmen and forefathers used to have there, we will all follow you. But if you will not follow what we farmers say, then we shall go against you and kill you and not put up with disturbance and law-breaking from you.' One notes the atmosphere and perceives the legal possibility of the Thing, the only one it had against a turbulent king; to threaten to kill him if he would not bow to the will of the people.

Here at the Thing the judicial influence of the people, which was by no means slight, was developed. A king had to be accepted by every provincial Thing. In Denmark the pretender to the throne, who was usually the son of the deceased ruler, had first to go to the Viborg Thing, where he was lifted up on to a large stone. After that he received the homage of the other provincial Things. But these Things did not lose sight of the king's politics, and sometimes made good their threat to throw out a king who had no luck, e.g. one who was unsuccessful.

Illustration on previous page: the Vikings had an eye for a beautiful but also dramatic landscape. They were agreed that Thingvalla was the best setting for the Icelandic Althing. Here the Thing-farmers met; they came riding up on their little horses and were glad to meet relatives and friends—and also no doubt an enemy or two, who might be provoked. For the duration of the Thing, however, there had to be no resort to force and weapons. From the high law-rock, the laws were recited, and it was not unusual for the fate of Iceland to be decided here. Christianity was established here by law in the year 1000, and in such a way that civil war was avoided. In the evening tales were told; to meet was also to exchange poems and stories. Thingvalla is a magnificent landscape which even today has lost none of its powerful effect.

This expressive but obscure scene from a Gotland picture-stone appears to illustrate the dead warrior's journey into the other world. He floats above an eight-legged horse, Sleipner, while three warriors hold their swords pointing downwards in front of them.

The ordinary Things, for a hundred or a *birk,* had enough to do in the form of antagonisms between people. Self-vindication belonged to the age. The times for meeting seem to have been fixed at new moon and full moon, but there might have been others. At any rate the time was known to all, and free men fit to bear arms gathered at the Thing-place. There had to be a minimum number present at the hearing of cases, but we cannot reckon that anyone other than the inner circle of experienced men gave utterance. In Sweden, Norway and Iceland they had a special law-man, who knew the laws, and it is conceivable that he went through the laws once a year. Thanks to their very memorable phrasing, it was possible to recite them and teach people to apply them in practice.

Any kind of proper trial does not seem to have been embarked upon. Proof of innocence was adduced by agreeing on a witness who guaranteed that one was innocent. The Thing only had to ensure that the accused either produced such a witness or, if this could not be done, paid a fine. Otherwise, a serious lawbreaker had to be outlawed, which was for life, or banished for three years. The men of the Thing gave an audible demonstration that they were agreed by rattling their weapons *(vapnatac;* a term used in England, moreover, for a northern district that came under a Thing).

The Thing was thus a popular authority which had great influence over the existence of every family and every man, and the laws themselves had been formed by people's ordinary way of thinking; but it was the tight circle of Thingsmen on the Thing-logs who held forth.

The common man did not join in the discussions with words; had he
done so, meetings would have degenerated into idle gossip. Wherever
there was a leading figure, or some of similar standing, their de-
liberations were close.

In Sweden, the law-man was a very prominent person. We have
evidence of this on a rune-stone set up by Jarlabanke, the great man
who said that he owned the whole of Täby. It informs us that he
'had this stone set up to himself in his lifetime, and made this Thing-
place; and he alone owned the whole of this hundred.' This may well
sound superior towards his contemporary Thing-farmers, but in any
case Jarlabanke was a man from the inner circle, undoubtedly a law-
man. It says nothing, after all, about what he did at the Thing; and
although he was a landed proprietor of some size, there is no indication that the farmers let themselves be subdued by him any more than
by a king.

It is typical that the Thing, which was part of the northerners' way
of life, went with them wherever they emigrated, which is shown by,
amongst other things, the wapentakes that are found in England.
Here their political ideas found expression, and here the blood of
more than one hotspur was cooled without the need for this to be

accompanied by revenge on his part against his assembled equals. The Thing-peace was strictly observed.

When Iceland was colonized, the need was felt after a time for an appropriate procedure which was suited to the particular locality. When this took place cannot be said for sure, but it must have begun already during the Viking period. What was new in Iceland was a common Thing for the whole country, the Althing, which was held in magnificent mountainous country east of Reykjavik, where the roaring River Öx flows down from Almannagjá into a lake. Here lay a piece of common-land, with space for huts for those who assembled from every direction on the days the Thing was held and spent the nights there. It was a welcome opportunity to meet and hear news. One listened to the tellers of sagas; relations saw each other again.

The Althing had a special court of law with 36 members, nominated by the priests (chieftains). On this point there are similarities with Denmark, for there too we meet the priest as religious and secular leader. The priests themselves, moreover, constituted an assembly that made laws; this, like other such matters, had to be done unanimously. The chief man—the leader of the Althing—proclaimed the new laws from a rock on the eastern side of the Almanna gorge, with a wide view over the valley.

The best known decision taken by the Althing was the adoption of Christianity. This occurred on June 24th in the year 1000, in a dramatic way. Thanks to Torgeir Gode, the Law-Speaker, the antagonisms that came close to splitting Iceland into two states were resolved. Himself a heathen, he gave the Thingsmen his analysis—after intense meditation for a whole day and night, lying under his fur in his hut. In this he stressed the calamity of dividing Iceland, and as an artful solution suggested that all who were still unbaptized should be baptized—but the putting out of babies and the eating of horsemeat should be allowed, as well as secret sacrifices to the gods. Sacrifices at which there were witnesses would be punished by banishment.

Iceland was divided into 36 *godords,* three of which made up a Thing-law. Each Thing-law held a hundred-Thing, led by the priests, one after the other in turn. Such a regular system was created only gradually, but it is interesting that a certain system of law in Scandinavia was used to build upon, and features were selected which fitted naturally into conditions in Iceland.

Ulvkel and Arnkel and Gye	They raised the stones
They made here a Thing-place.	And made the staff
Nor shall a memorial	The great one too
Greater be	As mark of honour.
Than the one Ulv's sons	Also Gyrid
Made after him,	Loved her mate.
Nimble fellows	A song of sorrow, then,
To their father.	Shall be his lay.
	Gunnar cut the stones.

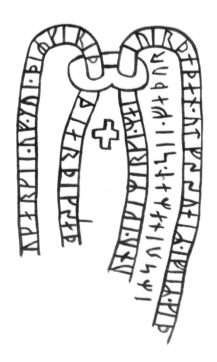

183

Profiles of Artists

When northerners met, the talk soon turned to experiences and memories. So they looked forward with pleasure to the meetings at the Thing, where they actually had a chance of seeing famous men and hearing story-tellers and *skalds*. They settled round them and forgot the time in order to listen. Here they saw the new fashions in clothes, exquisite swords and ornaments.

The poet and the artist-craftsman were well-regarded. The lays with their sure form spread far and wide from man to man, and brought fame to the subject of the song. We have met St. Olav's *skald,* Sigvat, who was a good support for the King. His poems won followers for the King and gave their stamp to people's idea of him. And the owner of noble ornaments and weapons was no less glorious. One suspects a mutual connection between the rhythmic succession of varied animal-motifs in a decorative band and that of the skilful words in their verse.

In the best works, the form gives a loftiness and purity to the meaning. An artist like Egil was certainly numbed by grief after the loss of his son, but he found relief in reciting his poetry. This far-away voice is genuine and human; we can feel its bitter tone like an urgent message right through its peculiar mode of expression:

> Slow does it go
> My tongue to stir,
> Nor am I able
> My words to weigh.
> It's no easy thing
> The gift of Odin
> Deep from the haunts
> Of the soul to draw.
>
> For the end is near
> Of my family line,
> Like trees of the forest
> Ravaged by storm.
> Nor is a man
> Merry in mood
> Who bears his son
> Away from the house.

Head of wood from a bed, found in the Gokstad grave. Note that in contrast to the animal-heads from Oseberg it has clearly marked whisker-lines on the muzzle.

Cruel was the hole
Torn by the sea
In my father's
Kinsmen's ranks.
Empty, I know,
It will be,
The place of my son,
Engulfed by the sea.

A noble gift
Had I of Odin:
The sport of verse
Without defect,
And such a cast
Of mind, I make
Of false friend
An open foe.

The Norsemen understood instinctively that words and pictures obtained secret power thanks to rhythm. The grave inscription which begins with a few reflective words becomes strong when it passes over into rhythm. Ragnhild's epitaph to Gunulv is remembered for these lines in the middle:

Few will now
Be better born

A proud memorial was given to the chieftain Toke by his *hird*-men:

Warriors raised
To their brother
The stone on the hill;
Firm it stands with runes.
They went nearest
Gorm's son Toke
He fled not
At Uppsala.

Early Nordic writing receives a special character from its terseness, and through negation a half-expressed thought can appear. A warrior is not said to be brave, but that he did not fly—implying that he went straight for the enemy, and did not weaken in the face of death. The effect is stronger than a direct statement.

To use expressions pregnant with meaning and link them rhythmi-

With power and voracity the beast of prey looks forth. There is a practised strength in this work—one of the four heads on the sledge in the Oseberg find, which received its name from the leader of the excavation, Gustafson. If one looks at it more closely, one discovers bird-motifs above the mouth with its bared teeth. The Viking Ship House, Bygdöy, Oslo.

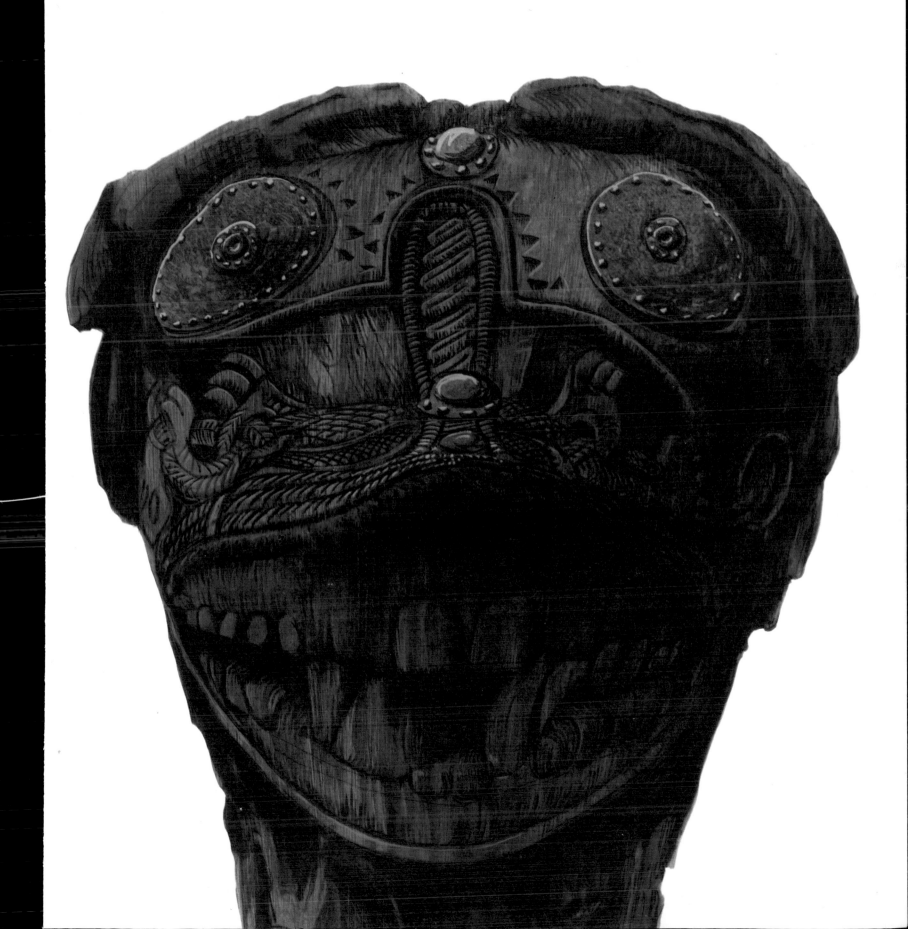

cally, to give force to alliteration and flight to kennings (poetic paraphrases), was not a matter for everyone. For the master, kennings in particular were a refined and ingenious means of expression. We came across this in discussing the many names for a ship (p. 11). Sailing was described fancifully as ploughing with the wet prow. The wolf was called the horse of the Valkyrie. An early Nordic poem and many runic inscriptions (from which these two expressions were taken) cannot be understood unless one knows the background to these kennings.

The alliteration reinforces the heavy rhythm and the terse expression. End-rhyming appeared only exceptionally in the poetry of the Viking era (on the Vallentuna stone) and then together with alliteration.

The content of the writing is given such marked form for the most part that we can hardly get through to the personality of the author. Egil we know, a capable Icelandic Viking who cunningly came through dangers in the British isles and escaped the vengeance of the Norwegian king, thanks to his ingenious verse. His thick-set figure stands, unshakable, in the memory, shrouded in the misty air of Iceland, weighed down with disappointments but with the proud look of a man born free. For later generations he is the man of the Viking epoch, completely and utterly.

A rich body of writing is preserved in Iceland, set down several centuries after its origin, but with many features from heathen times strangely alive. It bears witness to the particular abilities of the Icelanders, their interests and ideas, for instance, of the end of the world, *ragnarök*.

A wholly characteristic and masterly form is given to the subject in the Prophecy of Volvan, *Voluspa*. It is a consummate work, and like the lays of the *hird-skalds,* it would have lost its character if it had been altered in the course of time. It is also related to scaldic writing in mode of expression and line of thought, though it is hardly one of the *skalds* we know who stands behind this mighty poem. The end of the world is palpably evoked in an atmosphere of earthquakes and volcanic eruptions, which shifts between darkness and violent flashes of lightning, in order to ring out in sunny harmony in the new world.

The Prophecy of Volvan gives an interesting vision of people and gods as sprung from imperfect beings. The Æsir live recklessly, with gold in abundance. They let themselves be cheated into promising Frey, the sun and the moon to the giants, in return for having a new castle built. When it is built and the master builder wants his reward, the Æsir break their promise. This is a decisive moment. So not even the gods are perfect, after all, still less free from guilt. Odin has the chance to see into the future by drinking from Mimir's fountain. He looks into Ragnarök, the doom of the gods. The end here is given a

This Gotland artist had imagination and discovered how to show such animals as these, here rather worn, with feather-like offshoots. The animals on the hilt of the sword are seen partly through round holes, and partly the artist allows the surface to cover portions of the animals. State Historical Museum, Stockholm.

Obscure in details but consistent in its line of thought, The Prophecy of Volvan stands out as a strange work. Its creator was a man who knew life, a thinker and a visionary who was no stranger to either the good or the bad sides of people. His keynote is ethical. Those who are without guilt are the only ones to live on—just like Sigurd Fafnesbane. And yet evil, death and coldness exist, at the same time as, but separate from, the good, which is the proper goal. Those who receive a share of salvation from guilt enter also into immortality. 'A hall she sees (Volvan), more fair than the sun, decked with a golden roof, standing on Gimle (guardian of fire); there shall the host of guiltless live, to enjoy their bliss through all eternity.'

Thus high did the thoughts of the Norsemen soar, and yet there was at the same time a clear tendency to choose moderation and the middle way, in order to be on the safe side of existence. This is given its clearest expression in Havamal, the words of the High One, which also contains, moreover, profound religious writing. Here too the emphasis is on the good man. Its sayings correspond completely with usages we know from rune-stones. Thus a Swedish inscription from Ivla in Småland draws up its tribute in almost the same words as Havamal:

> Gentle with his people.
> Liberal with food.
> By all
> Much praised.

Havamal contains a veritable handbook on how to live. It emphasizes the joy of having possessions, even if they are small, so long as one is independent. So as not to get into a fix, one should be silent, tactful and distrustful. Only in tried friends can one put one's trust. Rise early and be industrious, do not drink too much ale and refrain from seeming too wise! The moderate man is the most carefree.

As with the generous man, praise is given to the hospitable. Without a well-disposed reception at the farms, the wayfarer was badly placed, tired and dirty as he had become towards nightfall. Sigvat felt hurt when he was refused accomodation, merely because the farm people did not want to house him at a time when they were holding a sacrifice. Havamal knows the situation:

> Fire needs he
> Who's just come in
> With cold about his knees;
> Food and clothes
> Are the need of the man
> Who's fared across the mountain.

Parts of the Oseberg ship, with the varying figure-of-eight animals, who twine into each other. The Viking Ship House, Bygdöy, Oslo.

191

Such diverse subjects were mastered by the *skald,* from those near at hand to the visionary, and it is characteristic that it was undoubtedly an Icelander who composed the memorial to the Danish sea-king at Karlevi on Öland, a magnificent lay in regular *dróttkvaett.* He is mentioned as a warrior by artificial expressions such as helper of the war-goddess. And as a sea-captain, he was called by the name of a sea-king (Åndill) + *iarmundgrund* (=wide area) + *reid*-Vidurr (wagon-Odin), i.e. mighty ship's leader on the wide sea ('wagon of the sea' is a ship).

With this language of analogies, artistically mastered, the poet could pay the generous king magnificent homage. And who did not want to have his memorial tribute so worded that he was saved from slipping down among the villains?

The *skald,* like the artist-craftsman, moved from one great man to another and let himself be wooed. Loyalty among these gifted men was no doubt a virtue, but hardly a general practice. The best of them were lured by gold rings and other desirable objects. Sigvat, too, felt drawn to others for a time, but after King Olav's serious reminder he acknowledged after all that it was with him that he belonged.

The ends of the Oseberg wagon, like the rest of the body, are adorned with highly effective woodcarvings. On the left of this end is a definite scene: Gunnar in the snake-pit. He is being bitten by a reptile and is trying to defend himself. All round, the surface is filled with ribbon-animals clutching each other. Here is an example of how the Nordic artist created the 'clutching beast' from a palpable motif. It is an original and valuable representation.

Wagons of this type were in common use and are known from, amongst other things, the Gotland picture-stones, see p. 160. The Oseberg wagon was no doubt used specifically for journeys in style. Compared with ships, the vessels of the land-routes were slower, but hardly less capricious. The Viking Ship House, Bygdöy, Oslo.

This circle of great men attracted capable wood-carvers and other artist-craftsmen. We can see their work in the Norwegian Oseberg grave, a collection of outstanding pieces from the first half of the 9th century. The masters who made them are a whole group of different artistic personalities. In the grave, which was covered by an imposing mound, stood the well-preserved Viking ship—which we have already met (p. 61)—and in the ship, an abundance of burial gifts. The most precious had been stolen, but the wooden objects, on the other hand, were untouched, including a wagon, some sledges and beds, posts with animal-heads, and some less finely decorated equipment. The woman who was laid to rest in the chamber in the middle of the ship was a prominent, art-loving Maecenas, who was magnanimous enough to attach to herself completely different artist-craftsmen, not only those recognised as the best, but also wood-carvers with a more debatable style.

The ship itself is a work of art. The two end-posts are elegantly decorated; one terminates in a spiral-coiled snake with a broad head, and on both sides of the prow are carved reliefs, wide rhythmic bands of closely interlaced animals with almost figure-of-eight bodies, from which the heads and limbs extend. No two of these flat animals are alike, only the basic pattern and the composition are the same. Each animal has its particular features. If one looks more closely, one

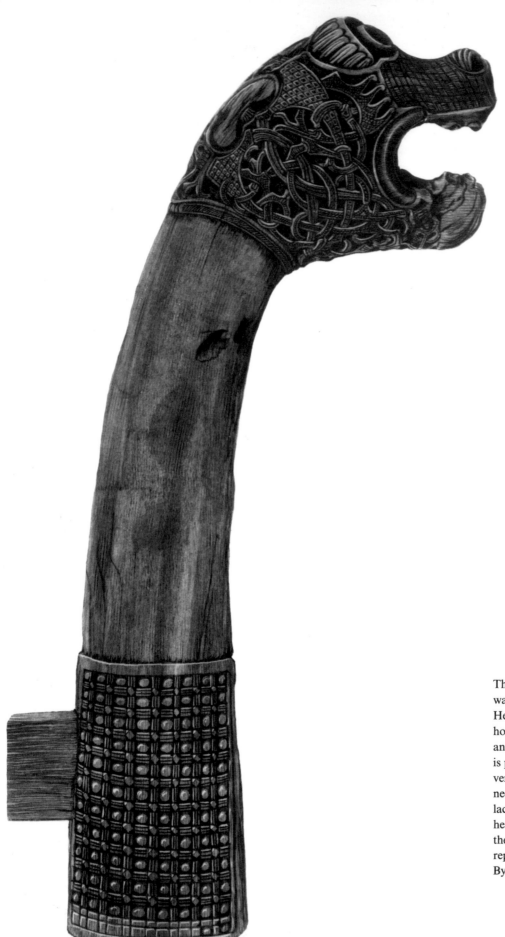

The wood-carver who made this animal-head post was christened the Academician by Hakon Shetelig. He is skilful, careful over every detail, and understood how to give smooth parts, geometric ornaments and animal-motifs an elegant effect side by side. He is probably the surest of all the Oseberg wood-carvers, but not on the other hand the most original. It needs a practised eye to be able to follow the interlaced creatures below the eye of the gaping animal-head. The Vikings found it no easier to understand the art of their time than we do the advanced representations of today. The Viking Ship House, Bygdöy, Oslo.

Christ on the cross has stretched out his huge arms in a comprehensive gesture. In spite of all his humility, he represents the triumph of Christianity. Detail from the great Jelling stone.

The Urnes style, which may be studied on this very beautifully decorated rune-stone from Skråmsta in Haga, Uppland, is also a further development of the ribbon-animal. Little snakes, whose heads are seen full-face, coil themselves round the large animal.

no quarter was given in the demands made on him. Some time between 965 when Harald was baptised and 985 when he died, the artist received the commission, chose the sides of the stone for each of his representations, and began cutting.

One side shows Christ on the cross. His figure stands stiff and flat amongst the loops of ribbon-work, which wind about freely. Some run out into tendrils. Christ holds his arms outstretched. There is

This gilded bronze weather-vane from Heggen, Modum, in Norway, is a noble and artistic piece of work. It was set at the mast-head of a Viking ship, but one must really hope that the mast was lowered so often that the crew could enjoy its details and admire the scene, with the two fanciful animals with acanthus leaves instead of tail and mane. The weather-vane is a fine representative of late Viking art in the Ringerike style. University Collection of Antiquities, Oslo.

power in the gesture but little slits across the eyes show that He is dead. Such shallow incisions were presumably shown up with colour, like the main motif.

More stately is the other side with the lion, the most magnificent animal of the Mammen style. In spite of its slender head, with whiskers and a neck that breaks out into an extravagant acanthus, the animal is majestic. The feet end in huge claws. Its bearing is proud in its struggle with the snake, which winds insidiously about its body. Together they show how intense and imaginative the artist was; he had certainly never seen a lion. On the other hand, he was familiar with earlier animal-figures in Viking art and probably also knew pictures of lions in foreign art. On the Jelling stone he unites foreign motifs—the lion and Christ—with traditional resources of expression and produces a particularly original work. The stereotyped Christ-figure is surrounded by stylised plants. The animal struggling with the serpent—an ancient motif, even in Nordic ornamentation—acquires a deeper significance. The serpent obviously represents Evil. Acanthus from Christian art grows together with Nordic animal-limbs in an amazing way. While plant motifs had been avoided in earlier Viking art, artists now took them up, but in accordance with their own imagination.

This symbiosis of animals and plants continues in the Ringerike style, represented with particular richness in Norway, in the country-side north of Oslo. In relation to the animals of the Jelling stone, the shoots are stylised and drawn-out. Also taken from the acanthus leaf

One of the most distinguished examples of the gold-smiths' craft that we know from the Viking age are the spurs from Röd, Östfold, in Norway. They are executed in fine Borre style; the amusing animal-heads and characteristic interlacing in a chain-pattern show the particular nature of the style. Such rich equipment, gold filigree and granulation, can only have belonged to a king or great chieftain. University Collection of Antiquities, Oslo.

is a simplified detail, the pear-shaped lobe, and from the Mammen style a distinctively stylised tree, which shoots up like a creeper from a double spiral. A fine example of this showy style is the decoration on the weather-vane from Heggen, the triangular metal plate at the top of the mast of a Viking ship. It shone all around and drew attention to itself. The best work in the Ringerike style outside the north is the relief on a sarcophagus that was found in the centre of London (see p. 29). It has a runic inscription and was evidently intended for a man of Nordic origin.

Viking art comes to an end with a very thin *fin-de-siècle* ornamentation, the Urnes style. It is as though it had lost its original force and become just a game with lines. Exaggeratedly graceful animals on the western end of the church at Urnes cover the whole of its surface. They form, however, an effective, undulating rhythm—slender bodies and limbs swing, swell and sway, so that one is nonetheless fascinated. The whisker-loops have become completely stylised, an independent flourish. The eye takes up most of the head.

The technical mastery is still there, but it lacks exuberance. It is no wonder that the Romanesque style with its fabulous creatures and motley world completely took the wind of the anaemic Urnes animals. The churches and monasteries supplied fresh tasks and promised good payment. Behind them they had the king—whose memorial stone at Jelling was an entirely heathen conception—and they presented a wealth of motifs and vivid episodes.

With the Urnes style, Viking art faded out. Nordic motifs still held their own for a time in the British Isles, especially in Ireland, and then disappeared even there. From now on Norsemen, like everyone else, followed international taste.

It might be imagined, perhaps, that Viking art was grey and hard to interpret. But numerous finds show that natural colours were used —blue, red, white—both on the decorated stones and on the wood-carvings. The colours were used to accentuate details, such as eyes or parts of the body, and even runic words were painted in, so as to reveal them more clearly. There was, in fact, a delight in gaudy colours, which gave pleasure in those days and drew attention to themselves.

The out-of-the-way little church at Urnes (see map p. 122), through the doubtless well-founded thrift of the inhabitants, has retained to a large extent its original condition and not been exposed to any rebuilding in a style more typical of the time. The slender animals wind about each other almost fondly, refined, indeed downright degenerate. Such was the evolution of the Viking style towards the end of the era. It is named after this church, and one is seized with admiration for the masterly skill of the wood-carver. Even here, away in an isolated part of Norway, such fine things as this could be made. What may not have been produced then in the districts where the king and other great men attended divine service?

The carving, which represents the most dramatic incidents in the life of Sigurd Fafnesbane (see text), is no less than 4.7 m. long. The whole of the drama is summarized here in a concentrated rune-and-picture engraving, which yielded its meaning without difficulty to those who knew the fantastic account from the poems or stories. The runic inscription has no direct connection with the pictures. It relates that 'Sigrid built this bridge. (She) was Orm's daughter . . .' The carving is on a smooth, inclined rock-face at Ramsund in the parish of Jäder, near Eskilstuna, Sweden.

He ought to eat it himself, then he would become the wisest one of all.' The second said: 'There lies Regin, who will betray the one who trusts him most.' The third thought Sigurd should kill Regin and keep the treasure, the fourth that he should ride to Brynhild, the fifth that he would be foolish if he spared Regin now that Fafnir had been killed.

Sigurd took the good advice, cut off Regin's head, ate the dragon's heart, and collected as much of the gold as Grane could carry.

Impressive passages from this legend are depicted on the Ramsund Rock in Södermanland. The main characters can be seen at the decisive moments. The huge border with the runic inscription is Fafnir himself. The dragon's body is pierced from below by Sigurd. Tied to the tree in the middle stands Grane, and sitting in its branches are the birds. Sigurd is holding Fafnir's heart over the fire and listening (clearly stressed) to their song. On the far left lies Regin, his head severed from his body. The smith's tools lie beside him: bellows, anvil, hammer and the tongs. It did not bother the spectator steeped in mythology that the fire over which Fafnir's heart is roasting could be burning in the smithy.

The Ramsund carving bears the imprint of the style of its time, the Ringerike, and interestingly enough, there is a considerably poorer version of the same motif in the vicinity, a copy. This shows a thing we see time and again—that alongside the outstanding works of art simpler imitations sprang up. The great artist was expensive to employ, but there were artist-craftsmen with lesser ambitions who made things cheaply and quickly.

The gods themselves played a living part in the Norsemen's imagination. They were down-to-earth personalities, but on a grand scale, who were evidence of their worshippers' ideals. Often depicted on the Gotland picture-stones is Odin's swift horse with eight legs, Sleipnir. One cannot be sure, however, that it is always just the god who is riding it. One of Sleipnir's tasks was to carry the dead to Valhalla, to eternal, joyous battle and the feasting so relished by the warriors. On one picture-stone a human figure is seen lying above the horse's back, and near by, with their backs towards it, three men with down-turned swords (see p. 181). One gets the impression that

There can be no doubt that this detail from a stone cross on the Isle of Man illustrates a heathen incident from mythology. It may be Odin who is being devoured by the Fenris-wolf. He defends himself with his spear and a raven sits on his shoulder. The knotted snake was a popular motif.

The rider on the eight-legged horse—probably Sleipner, Odin's courser—is received by the woman with the drinking-horn. Her long hair is tied in a knot at the neck and hangs down below it. She is dressed in a long skirt and shawl. Other figures can be seen in the background, and on the left, a strange building which has been interpreted as Valhalla. It has three doors and a domed roof. Is it perhaps the dead being welcomed or is it Odin himself returning? There are only pictures, no commentaries, on the Gotland picture-stones. This detail is from the stone at Alskog, Tjängvide.

this is a dead person who is about to be carried off. Odin was for many people the greatest god, the lord of battle and victory, but otherwise he is a dark figure, invested with no little mysticism. The Edda poems—which, as mentioned, were set down in Christian times—make him have visionary and ecstatic gifts. In Egil's Saga we learnt how Odin was thought to bestow the gift of poetry.

The most popular god—some considered him to be the greatest— was Thor. He is invoked in many runic inscriptions. In Adam of Bremen's account of the chief gods at Uppsala he sits in the middle. Reproductions of his hammer—with which he called forth lightning and thunder—were popular ornaments and supplanted only by the cross. He was a brave fighter, a little clumsy, but so overwhelmingly strong that everybody had to admire him. Who did not know the legend of his fight with the Midgard Serpent, depicted both on rune-stones and picture-stones? We have the whole description in an Edda poem, of how Thor went on a fishing trip with the giant Hyme. In order to have some bait he had taken the giant's bull and twisted off its head. Far out to sea Thor cast his hook, baited with the bull's head. The Midgard Serpent (which enclasped the world) took the bait. Thor then hauled in so powerfully that the serpent's head came into view, and he hit it with his hammer so that the mountains roared and the earth shook. At this the giant began to get worried. All he had gained from the trip was two whales; he persuaded Thor to head for home.

Pictures of this scene are known from the north to England. They are entirely to the Vikings' taste. On the Altuna stone in Uppland, Thor can be seen thrusting his foot through the bottom of the boat, so hard is he pulling. The subject otherwise has a more serious back-ground, the gods' settlement with the powers of evil, and this is repeated on a vast scale in the final battle, Ragnarök. It is quite likely that it was performed dramatically. We know from Adam of Bremen, a few years later, that the cult at Uppsala included singing and dancing. A mimed performance in addition to recitative is conceivable.

It may be worth quoting Adam's account, which is full of life but certainly not reliable about everything. He mentions that the people worship three statues of gods in a very famous temple: 'The most mighty of them, Thor, has his high-seat in the middle of the hall; Odin and Frey have their places on either side of him. Their characteristics are the following: "Thor", it is said there, "rules in the air and holds sway over thunder and lightning, wind and rain, good weather and the crops. The second, Odin, i.e. frenzy, conducts war and grants mankind bravery in face of the enemy. The third is Frey, who gives mortals peace and voluptuousness." His idol they also

The god of fertility, Frey, is depicted so clearly here that there can be no doubt about his identity. He sits with his pointed helmet and clutches his beard. This little bronze figure was found at Rällinge in the parish of Lunda, Södermanland. Height 7 cms. State Historical Museum, Stockholm.

The god Thor is portrayed here in bronze. He sits on a little chair and holds his hammer with both hands. The figure, ca. 7 cms. high, was found at Eyrarfjödur in Iceland. The National Museum, Reykjavik.

furnish with a huge phallus. Odin, on the other hand, they depict armed, just like Mars among us, while Thor with his sceptre seems to resemble Jupiter.'

This resemblance to the Roman gods appears also in the names for the days of the week. Tyr, the third great one among the Æsir, was the proper god of war. He gave his name to Tuesday, and was compared with Mars. Wednesday was Woden's (Odin's) or Mercury's day. Thursday, as the day of Thor and Jupiter, is again an indication that some regarded the God of Thunder as the highest. Frey, who belongs to the Gods of Fertility, the Vanir dynasty, was the god of crops, rain and sunshine (in Adam, Odin takes over some of the functions of this mild god). Together, the numerous Nordic gods, the Æsir and Vanir, cover the areas of power that were decisive for people's existence, the sky, the sea, war, crops, propagation and other functions, a little confusing at a quick run-through, but to believers worth worshipping and appeasing.

It was the business of the priests to make these powers well-disposed. They functioned in a district or a province. The king acted as a rallying-point for the whole people, and occasionally they gathered for great festivals. Lejre in Denmark and Uppsala in Sweden were important sanctuaries. Adam of Bremen describes the forms of worship at the latter: 'If there is a threat of epidemics and famine, sacrifices are made to the idol Thor; if war, to Odin; and if a wedding is to be celebrated, to Frey. Likewise it is customary every ninth year to hold a common festival at Uppsala for all the Swedish provinces... The king and ordinary people, one and all, bring their gifts to Uppsala ... The sacrifice takes place in the following way: of all living creatures of the male sex, they sacrifice nine, with the blood of which it is the custom to appease the gods. But the bodies are hung up in a grove that lies near the temple. This grove, namely, is so sacred to the people that every tree in it is considered to be divine because of the death and putrefaction of the sacrifices. Here dogs and horses hang together with humans, and a Christian told me that he had seen 72 bodies hanging beside each other. Furthermore, the songs that are usually sung on this occasion are so many in number and so unseemly that it is best not to speak of them.' Although Adam has obviously not seen the famous sacrificial grove, but has his knowledge of the heathen religion from northern Christians, he gives an important glimpse into a strange, last phase of heathenism. We find ourselves in its last period, when it was being driven back by Christianity but was making a last attempt to assert itself, also influenced probably by the new faith. An addition to the manuscript from about the same time states that 'for nine days they hold ritual meetings and perform sacrifices of this kind. Every day they sacrifice a human being together

The picture-stone from Lärbro, Tängelgårda, Gotland, exhibits some remarkable details, such as this group of people flourishing their drinking-horns outside and inside a framed scene. Two men raise their knives over the sack-like object. Hanging down from their arms are presumably folds of their cloaks.

with some animals, so that in nine days 72 living creatures are sacrificed. This sacrifice takes place around the vernal equinox.'

Of Lejre, Thietmar tells us a hundred years earlier, but in equivalent circumstances, that 'every ninth year they gathered in the month of Januari and celebrated Yule by, amongst other things, sacrificing 99 humans and as many horses to their gods, besides dogs and cocks, and also hawks.' He too received his information from others. It is with reservations, therefore, that one makes use of these sources, just as one does of the important records that have been preserved of smaller and more everyday ritual meetings. During a communal meal with food and ale, strength was derived from the gods. People raised cups and wished each other a good year. Meat from the sacrificial animals was prepared in roasting-pits and eaten. A dramatic, perhaps not wholly reliable account exists of a sacrificial meal in

Brooch-pin from Valbo, Gästrikland, Sweden, probably for a penannular brooch. It is finished with a fantastic creature, a man in the guise of a bird, or a bird in the guise of a man. Ca. 4.5 cms. State Historical Museum, Stockholm.

which the Christian Hakon Adelstensfoster had to take part. He was forced to bend over the sacrificial cauldron and got the taste of fat in his mouth. They accused him of making the sign of the cross instead of the hammer symbol, and so there was displeasure on both sides.

At the banquets vows were made about great exploits. One word led to another in the excited atmosphere, and a Viking soon found himself obliged to carry out deeds as full of honour as they were dangerous. It seems, moreover, that omens were consulted by casting lots as to one's destiny.

During all this a spontaneous feeling of community arose, with each other and with the gods. A singular element in religious life was the *sejd,* practised by women and men with neurotic symptoms. They can be compared most readily with the shamans of Siberia, and were both feared and loathed. During sessions they went into a trance; the soul left the body, it was said, and travelled freely.

As a religion, heathenism played a fundamental part in society; but although everyone gathered under the leadership of the king— he was indeed the people's source of luck—this obviously happened quite rarely. The cult was pursued mostly in small groups at home. Its peculiar importance for the family lay in ancestor worship. It is characteristic that while Christianity gradually drove out heathenism, the worship of ancestors continued. And even if the families' protective spirits gave up their ancient places, they were seen by the converts at the time of parting as real and dangerous. As a soughing in the air they swept past the farms, where the inmates took cover under the low roofs, in anguish for revenge.

For the heathen, a burial was an expression not only of grief, but also of a number of protestations and assurances, for the deceased as well as for the survivors. Existence continued after death, only in a different way. No wonder some people wished their dead ones would 'enjoy the grave well,' that they would feel at peace there and not obtrude into the circle of the living. Although the departed might be good, there was also the possibility that they represented malevolence and vindictiveness. At all events one had to secure them the peace of the grave. This was one of the reasons why on the grave-stones curses were laid on those who took the rune-stones away, and why they were promised all kinds of atrocities, such as being bewitched by *sejd* or being turned into a *räde,* a *sejd*-man. But unfortunately people did not hold off. Many of the richest graves have been plundered, undoubtedly for the sake of gain. Thus we have heard how Vikings with spade in hand looked for good spoils in Irish graves. They were no less enterprising at home. When one of the women laid to rest in the Oseberg grave lacks an arm, which in all probability bore valuable rings, this is surely a sign of a precipitate theft. Large graves such as

Jelling and Ladby have been plundered, which must have taken quite a long time. One cannot understand how it was tolerated. It is without doubt to be ranked with other forms of loot, and at times yielded magnificent returns.

The background to this, of course, is that a full outfit was laid down with the dead. It was recognised that they had needs on a par with those of the living. Although the burial gifts could not fill a continuing want, they were at least on hand during a transition period, perhaps until the dead had reached their final destination. They were given food and drink in vessels, but this was not enough for more than one or two meals. On the other hand, they had their clothes, and the freeman his weapons and sometimes a horse and dog. Harness became particularly common during the 10th century, after the appearance of regular cavalry. In the same way, women wore their rings and bead necklaces, their breast ornaments and the two oval brooches. The poor had with them only their knives; the mighty were laid in a chamber or in their ship with all their wealth of gold and silver, glass beakers and vessels. The Oseberg grave gives only

The Norseman's imagination was full of fabulous beings and supernatural features. What to us is natural—like flying—was sorcery to the Vikings. Here, the Gotland picture-stone from Lärbro, Stora Hammar, shows a man in feathered guise.

There is a notably powerful and gloomy atmosphere about this meeting. The woman welcomes the rider with uplifted drinking-horn and their eyes bind them together. He sits well-armed, and dressed in baggy, half-length trousers, on his horse, which trots along briskly. She wears a long dress down to her feet. It is an expressive and intense scene. Such was the subtlety of the Gotland artist in composing his figures on the picture-stones. From Halla, Broa.

216

the everyday side of such a great man's environment. We must imagine that it also contained ornaments of the same perfect quality as the golden articles from Röd in Norway.

These great people sometimes had a retainer with them in the grave, so as to have help in the many situations in which they were accustomed to have a slave at their disposal. By the Oseberg woman lay another woman. At her command, moreover, she had several horses, which must also have been killed at the burial. Provisions were provided for all of them. There is no denying it—the preparations for such a journey of the dead were barbaric and horrible.

In the south mound at Jelling one or two strange details are preserved which in part lead one to think of the exotic burial rites in

Bulgar described by Ibn Fadlan. In the middle of the mound stood a large pole, and at the top there were post-holes for a square building. We come across such traces of a pole set up in the middle of a burial-mound from other periods during the Iron Age. Alongside the standing-stones *(bautastenar),* such wooden poles evidently had a part to play, both at the burial ground and the Thing-place (see p. 182). Many carvers of rune-stones are explicit in praising the multiple nature of the grave-memorial. At Stora Ryttern in Västmanland it says: 'Gudlev set the staff and these stones after Slagve, his son.' Beneath the south mound at Jelling there stood also two rows of *bautastenar,* as part of the original memorial. Both stones and staff obviously entered into the burial rites.

Matters are undoubtedly much the same with the traces of a building on the south mound. From other places, we know of remains of a small building on a grave. There is—as we shall see—a tradition down into Christian times, and even far into the 18th century there were 'houses of the dead' in Scandinavia, which were bound up with the cult of the dead. Almost right down to our own time, the ritual persisted in Karelia in which on certain days, first and foremost at midwinter, the great festival of the dead, food was placed in the house. It is possible that the Jelling building was of this nature; at any rate it would fit into the tradition that can be traced in the north. It was accepted that the dead had human needs and connections with the family. These began—after the actual funeral—with the burial ale, when the dead man was probably thought to be present, and continued with times of remembrance, first and foremost on mid-winter's night.

The burial grounds often lay close to the farms. We know of larger and smaller agglomerations of graves. They show that both cremation and interment occurred, sometimes at the same place. At Lindholm Höje, cremation was usual. This magnificent burial ground on Limfjord lies on a slope with a wide view. The graves are marked by settings of stones, some in the form of a ship; others are triangular, round or oblong. The ship-settings—those in Scandinavia are of imposing size—were not the least popular. They are mentioned on rune-stones, and apparently symbolized the mode of travel to the other world.

In time, a person's good name became strongly emphasized, the remembrance itself something full of consolation. This accords with the prominent position that was often given to the memorial stones. They sometimes lay like beacons, visible from far and around when one was steering for home shores. They were often set up by roads, those with plenty of traffic. Wayfarers stopped by the grave and remembered the departed.

The Gotland picture-stones exhibit a good many motifs whose significance was understood at once by people of that time but which to us seems obscure. Seen here is a procession—it could be conceived as a welcome to a home-coming warrior. The puffed-out trousers and the triangular bits of material—folds of cloak perhaps—which hang down from the arms are emphasized time after time in the pictures. Detail from picture-stone from Lärbro, Tängelgårda.

Such an imposing horn can hardly have been used by anyone but Heimdal. Figure from a stone cross on the Isle of Man.

Styrlög and Holm
Set up these stones
After their brothers
Next to the road.
They came to their end
On the way to the east.

Thorkel and Styrbjörn,
Worthy thanes.
Ingiger let rise
A further stone
After his sons,
A visible mark.

This inscription in half-stanzas, *fornyrdislag,* appears on a stone by a highway in Södermanland, and is only one of many that mention the roadside as a natural place for a memorial. Havamal expresses this in the same words:

Seldom do *bauta*-stones
Stand by the road,
Unless kin set them up to kin.

Even if the dead were not under them, never having come home from a Viking expedition, their names had to be commemorated. A child, therefore, was given the name of one of the eldest in the family, or of one who had just died, so that his soul could live on. The name was a living reality, and by being chiselled in imperishable material it acquired a share in eternity, at the same time as it gave the stone something of the departed's soul, his memory:

Rodsten and Eliv
Åke and Håkon,
The lads set up
After their father
A stately *kummel,*
To Kale, the dead.
So shall the memory
Of the good man live,
While the stone stands
And the staffs of the runes.

The same line of thought as this, on a rune-stone from Småland, is met with in Denmark, but it receives its strongest and most pregnant expression in Havamal:

Beasts die, kinsmen die,
One day you'll die too.
This I know that never dies:
The judgement o'er the dead.

Representations on the Gotland picture-stone from Alskog. Three details from the stone are on pp. 35, 104 and 160. The middle part of the picture-stone is damaged, and here we have made an attempt to reconstruct the picture.

The Holy Drott

The man who worshipped the Æsir and Vanir in all their multiplicity came up against the Christian, who honoured only one god, the ruler of men, the Holy Drott, as a rune-stone from Uppland puts it. But this sole god was not without helpers and intermediaries. God's mother stood by when it was a matter of leading converts to the heavenly light and paradise (the Risbyle stone). The Archangel Michael—coadjutor on the Last Day—was invoked, as well as other heavenly powers, and the saints. Particular supports were their own martyr-kings, such as St. Olav and St. Knut. Raised above the rather distracted period that preceded them, they appeared after their death as worthy instruments in the service of Christianity. The churches where they were buried, especially Trondheim, became much-visited by pilgrims, here ancestor-worship merged with the invocation of saints.

Many Norsemen had already turned their thoughts to the Christian teaching in foreign countries. They came to communities where it had acquired a standing. It was first and foremost the new arrivals who carried on violently or—like Thorgist and his wife—engaged in scandalous scenes in churches and convents. We have already met an archbishop, Odo of Canterbury, c. 940, who was of Danish origin. The Viking graves retain their character only during the first generations. People who came home from abroad were naturally enough susceptible to Christian influence.

In order to create a practical basis, with no obligations, for the heathens' journeys into Christian circles *primsigning* ('first-marking') was arranged: the heathen did not receive any kind of true baptism, but a symbol of the cross was made for him; later, when he got home, he may well have let the symbol pass for a Thor's hammer. In practice many Norsemen showed flexibility in their relations with Christianity. Rich foreign merchants and customers belonged to this

This crucifix from Birka is carried out in filigree and granulation, a popular technique during the Viking era. The crucifix is in fact only 4.7 cms. high. About the year 900. State Historical Museum, Stockholm.

223

religion. They wanted to live according to its message during their stays in the north. And one had to live together, after all, and do business with each other. During the first centuries, therefore, the Norsemen were quite obliging, allowing the Christians to build churches at Birka and Hedeby and letting missionaries function, probably mainly for the foreign merchants. But when the priests set to with great zeal, some with fanaticism, it eventually caused heathenism to resist. A certain practical attitude was maintained, however, which received its pregnant expression in the mould from Jutland that was used for both crosses and Thor's hammers. This reveals the enterprising goldsmith, who considered money from the Christian to be no different from heathen means of payment.

Later in the 10th century, the heathens had become sharply opposed to the Christian influence. The missionaries had certainly also made decisive progress. In Denmark, in about 985, the monk Poppo succeeded in converting King Harald Bluetooth, and with the king—the highest god of the gods—followed automatically responsibility for the well-being of the people. Although there were, of course, still many who were refractory or in direct opposition to the sanctioning of Christianity, all Christian priests obtained success. The conversion itself is typical, like that depicted by a contemporary Saxon chronicler, Widukind. It reveals no little of what people thought important. The King and Poppo argued about which god was the strongest, and when Poppo promised to demonstrate the power of Christ through the ordeal by fire, Harald agreed. The next day Poppo carried a large piece of iron, taken from the fire, for as long as the King wished. His hands received no injury. At this Harald ordered that Christianity, which had shown its incontrovertible power, should be the only religion and the ancient gods should be rejected.

In Norway and Sweden matters went more slowly. Here the opposition was bitter. Hakon Adelstensfoster (brought up at the court of the English king) made an attempt to convert Norwegian farmers. It is clear from the interesting account of it (p. 149) that it was in vain. Olav Tryggvason carried on fanatically and referred to the year 1000, near at hand, when the world was supposed to end. Tangbrand went to Iceland. There Christianity won such great success that the Althing realized that it was better to accept it than to divide the people. In Sweden, the bishop's seat was moved to Sigtuna after the fall of Birka, not to the heathen stronghold of Uppsala. Swedes made their way to Denmark, however, if they felt the need of Christianity. Many stones in Uppland commemorate baptismal journeys at the last moment. Obviously those about to die were filled with anguish in face of death, and turned to the church in order to 'get white clothes,' i.e. be baptised. 'Ingelev had this stone set up to Brune, her

The symbols replaced each other; after Thor's hammer came the cross, though this took place gradually. The silversmith who introduced the ornaments saw the advantage of being able to supply his wares both to the heathen who worshipped Thor and to the Christian who merely wanted a crucifix. It is characteristic, therefore, that a mould has been found at Trend in north Jutland which was used for both types, the hammer and the cross. The hammer in the picture is a Danish find, while the cross was found at Birka. The mould is 9.7 cms. long.

husband. He died in Denmark in white clothes. Balle cut (the runes).' So runs one of these very eloquent memorial inscriptions. But not only were the Christian powers beginning to be invoked on many rune-stones, the mode of expression itself changed completely. 'God help his spirit and soul better than he deserved.' 'May God help his spirit and soul, forgive his deeds and sins.' This is a different line of thought from the proud words that adorn the heathen rune-stones. Humility and consciousness of guilt penetrate the mental life. Now there is no consolation to be derived from a great name and an unforgettable memorial tribute. Only in the new faith is there hope.

In the course of the 11th century, heathenism gradually gives way. In the middle of the century Östman Gudfastsson boasts on a rune-stone at Fröson that he has Christianized Jämtland, and in about 1100 a church replaces the sacred grove and temple at Uppsala. The last conjurations to Thor, Odin and Frey can hardly have died away before Christian priests put the building in hand. With this the power of the gods disappeared for ever. Old Uppsala lies in a pathetic setting, with its row of heathen mounds of kings by the gloomy grove and the structures of the cult. But soon it was decreed by the law of Uppland: 'No one shall sacrifice to idols and no one shall put trust in groves or stones. All shall revere the church, to which all shall go, both the living and the dead, those who come into the world and those who go hence.' The church became the home of the dead. They had to rest there, even if the family still regretted being separated from the departed. Some found an outlet for their sense of affinity with their dead ones by raising a stone and building a sort of house-of-the-dead on the farm, like the people of Bogesund: 'Gunne and Åsa had this stone and chest of stone set up to . . . their son. He died at Ekerö. He is buried in the churchyard.'

The first object of the missionaries, once they had got a sure foothold, was to build churches. In the beginning they had to adapt themselves to the opportunities that were available in crowded market towns. Later, they aimed at making the building a monument worthy of the triumphant course of the faith. But they probably often lay outside the settlement. When the first church was built in Greenland, it was done in spite of the protest of Erik the Red and the constant perversity of his son Leif and his wife. They managed to get it erected a little way from the farm, close enough for one to be able to go to it easily, but still far enough away for it not to lie right in front of Erik's eyes. It was a simple little turf house, with room for a few people and with an altar opposite the entrance (see p. 75), rather like the reproduction of a very early church that we know from a Swedish stone. It is really only a chapel. Matters are much the same with the small churches in the British Isles and Ireland. Only with the growing influence of the priests and more ample financial means

A carving which shows a church and divine service. Inside the building crowned with a cross stands the priest, obviously at the altar. Outside—and perhaps partly inside the building—are the assembled people. It recalls Irish-Scottish chapels and also conditions in the turf-church at Brattahlid. The stone is at Sika, in the parish of Frötuna, Uppland, Sweden.

for building were churches constructed of stone or with beautifully scoured staves and beams.

The best-known Norwegian stave-church, the beginning of a fine series of wooden churches, is Urnes. Its ornamentation is completely in the traditional style, as we have seen (p. 205), uninfluenced by the Romanesque Christian art. In the foundations of the present stave-church are traces of an older church building of smaller size, to which the carved pieces of wood evidently belong. It is hardly five metres wide, rectangular, with traces of an outer cloister, and with a square apse. In the middle, four pillars clearly supported a slightly higher central tower, which effectively indicates that it is no ordinary building.

In the same way we see, time after time, beneath the stone churches of southern Scandinavia, traces of pillars and staves from the mission churches before the Romanesque stone buildings. Especially interesting are Hörning (Djursland) and Jelling. The former is built on top of a Viking mound and suggests a connection between the grave-cult of Viking times and the founding of churches. In the mound was a square chamber with rich equipment of a typical kind, amongst other things the table mentioned earlier (p. 152). Above this, a stave-church had been constructed later, after the mound had been levelled

The tapestry from Skog provides one of the most peculiar testimonies to the atmosphere which prevailed among the Christians, who felt threatened by evil forces from without. They moved into the church and the belfry. Here they rang the bells with all their might and protected themselves with prayers and signs of the cross. The building was adorned with terrifying animal-heads, to judge by this simple representation, and perhaps a pair of birds have settled on the roof, they too in search of security. Detail, after the tapestry, 165 cms. long and 45 cms. wide, which is in the State Historical Museum, Stockholm.

The Christian idea permeates many of the early representations on the stone crosses on the Isle of Man. Here a man of God is seen with the cross in one hand and the Scriptures in the other, surrounded by two snakes, which hardly symbolize the good, and a fish.

off a bit, without destroying the grave. Amongst the objects in it is a piece of wood preserved with carved Urnes animals, beautifully executed, and painted in red and brown.

Jelling was for a time the preferred seat of the kingly power. There must have been a royal demesne there, and on it, Gorm and Tyra were laid to rest in a massive monument which included two large mounds. One of them is empty but covers two diverging rows of standing-stones. In the other mound was a large chamber of wooden staves. A number of carved wooden objects come from the chamber. Above it lay a little silver goblet, which had obviously been dropped during the plundering of the grave. It is conceivable that the chamber was the resting place of Tyra and Gorm (it was divided across the middle by a plank). To this extent it is a purely heathen structure, like the little rune-stone there, set up by King Gorm to Tyra. The great Jelling stone is the work of the son, Harald. With it Christianity was introduced, and it suggests—which seems to conflict with its sentiment—that Harald had made the monument to his parents. Presumably, however, he also built the first stave-church on the site, so that his Christian intentions came out into the open. It was replaced by a building which rested on a thick stone footing, and far later, the last version of the church went up, stone-built and imposing.

The Christianizing of the north took place without many dramatic episodes. Here and there hotheads carried on violently, but for the most part the change was marked by quiet thoughtfulness. The Icelandic Law-Speaker's careful weighing of the strength and future prospects of the two trends of belief was very characteristic. Christianity held a steady course and moved forward purposefully. The priests, right from the first missionary, Willibrord, around the year 700, bought slave-boys and reared them in the Christian faith. They used on the whole no little money and valuables to free people from slavery, and this naturally made a number of people well disposed. The use of his personal possessions—like Rimbert (see p. 168)—came more naturally to the Christian than to the heathen. And yet this might well go too far, as is borne out by the Bishop of Winchester. He had to write to Count Arnulf of Flanders, who had a band of Vikings in his service, and ask for the return of an evangelistary, which two clerics had sold without his knowledge so as to be able to redeem a little girl from 'your Danes.' The Norsemen themselves were not so sensitive on this point. Dealing in slaves was one of the most profitable professions.

The whole of the great mass of poor people must have felt drawn to Christianity, but it was through the chieftains, and first and foremost the kings, that the missionaries worked and acquired their influence. In return, the people transferred the special regard which the *godes* had enjoyed to the priests, not always to their benefit. Thus

227

Pope Gregory later had cause to complain that the Danes held the clergy responsible for bad times, bad weather and all sorts of maladies. Swedes and Goths—according to the well-known English author Ailnoth—accused the priests of being behind crop failures and other set-backs. Deep-seated habits of thought were not to be shaken off without difficulty.

This applied above all to ancestor-worship, which was a self-evident part of the Norsemen's world of thought. Although the priests invited the dead to the churches, with them came also the cult of the dead, which was connected in part with the old burial grounds.

It has been mentioned elsewhere (p. 218) that there had been a sort of house-of-the-dead in prehistoric times. Such small buildings above the ground were erected also as memorials and in church-yards. Notable are the chests from Eskilstuna, which were not by any means supposed to house the dead but to stand on top of the graves and were, amongst other things, places for the cult of the dead. The ends were made of high stones, which, in conformity with the long sides, were decorated with animal motifs. Runic inscriptions had been cut into the stones.

Even after the conversion of the Norsemen, many time-honoured ways of thought survived; these formed a part of a view of reality which could not be altered without the loss of something essential to existence. One can exchange one's gods for a stronger divine power, but one cannot dispense with the feeling of affinity within the family, a feeling which embraces the living as well as the dead.

Old Uppsala was one of the main heathen centres in the north. In its dismal grove, humans and animals were sacrificed to satisfy the demands of the gods. The Church came late to the strongest citadel of heathendom, but when it came it prevailed also over the whole country.

Reality and Fantasy

Every attempt to describe a prehistoric society builds on fragments. The further away in time it lies, the fewer are the facts at our command. One can pass over, as far as possible, whatever is lacking, but one thing and another will have to be filled out for the sake of coherence. Some things one can get at by analogies, others perhaps from later sources—both procedures are risky.

The Icelandic family sagas have coloured many people's idea of the Viking era; but although their characters are from that time, the sagas reflect another, later world of thought. They do, on the other hand, fulfil all the requirements of *belles-lettres:* dramatic action, sharply-drawn characterizations, and a masterly style.

In all essential matters we have kept to the contemporary evidence and laid weight on the archaeological discoveries and the runic inscriptions. Only to a limited extent have chronicles and annals been used. They suffer from strong and understandable prejudices, recorded as they were by the Vikings' adversaries, people of the church. Under their pens minor forces turn into armies, attacks on monasteries into murder, fire and annihilation, and extorted taxes into fantastic sums. Nevertheless, they have preserved vivid and undoubtedly authentic glimpses into the way of life of the time, in biographies such as those of Ansgar and Rimbert.

The Thing-place on the Isle of Man, Tynwald Hill, is a terraced mound built up of turfs. Here the Vikings assembled, and their successors down to the present day, to discuss law and problems of justice. The Thing, with its characteristic functions, is a part of the Viking era which has preserved itself tenaciously through modern times and held its own against a remote parliament in London.

Two sources have been used as being particulary reliable, because they reveal a strong tradition: Place-names and the poems of the historically-known *skalds*. The latter are executed with such ingenious mastery that they can hardly have suffered any essential alterations in the copies that have been preserved to us. The texts connected with the poetry, on the other hand, are obviously made up fundamentally from the poems. Some are quite as unreliable as many contemporary sources, e.g. the Arabian ones. Although part of what these tell us seems amazingly authentic, there are other things that by no means fit into the picture of the Norseman that one has been able to form from more reliable sources. It prompts the downright question whether the Rus people who are mentioned were in fact Vikings, or whether they were perhaps a people from the north who had migrated from Scandinavia earlier and, in a foreign country, had acquired new customs. With the help of grave finds one can establish that between Onega and Ladoga a population existed which was related to the Scandinavian, and which at least had characteristics from there. Although we may notice, therefore, certain features that are related to the Nordic ones (e.g. ship burial, posts in burial mounds), there are also wholly exotic elements (e.g. the imported harem system, the large, green glass beads for the ships, unknown in the north, people's dirtiness and shameless customs), which seem partly invented. It is really not surprising that these Arabian sources conflict with each other in many respects. The description of the Norsemen at home also offers such amazing statements (the worship of Sirius, etc.) that one dare not put confidence in them in every detail.

Right, Gaut's cross in Kirk Michael on the Isle of Man. On the stone it says in runes: 'Melbrigdi, son of Adakan the smith, raised this cross for his . . . soul, Gaut made this and all on Man.' Gaut Björnsson lived in a place called Kuli—presumably Cooley in the parish of Michael. The cross on the ring-chain which is named after Gaut is carried out in Borre style, and this can be recognized as from north-west England, which is no doubt where Gaut had come from. But, like the artist's family, the style derives from Scandinavia.

To the left of Gaut's cross is a fragment of a stone cross with animal ornamentation in the Mammen style. The patterns are well-known from wood-carvings and are translated into the soft slate-stone on the Isle of Man. The stone was raised by the Viking Odd in Kirk Bradden.

The illustrations on the next two pages are also from the Isle of Man. Above left, a well-armed Viking, as portrayed on one of the stone crosses.

The right-hand picture is also from a stone cross. It may be a priest that appears in this detail. Below him stands a saddled horse, tied up.

Bottom left, a captured or hanged man. Detail from a gravestone.

However important the archaeological evidence may be, it has to be interpreted to mean anything, and even carefully considered interpretations can be misleading. Discussion of the coins began before anything else, and they yielded much important evidence. We have used them here and there for commercio-political and cultural assessments.

Of the finds, naturally none are more significant than the human skeletons, but even they have been the object of shifting views. Thus the Norsemen in Greenland have been regarded as partially degenerate, but in the light of the latest researches at Brattahlid, this was obviously not the case. On the contrary, it was a vigorous population that was laid to rest by the humble church. Of the 144 buried, 23 were children, who had nearly all died at a tender age. The men seldom got to more than fifty; the women more often reached sixty. Many suffered from gout. The Norsemen had strong teeth and were powerfully built, but the simple dwellings, often damp and chilly, were insanitary. Deformed backs or hips are fairly common, and the same applies to skeletons found in Scandinavia. They had difficulty, of course, in keeping an even heat all winter—not to mention spring and autumn. The open hearth gave only radiant heat, like a very simple stove. Although the well-off procured down quilts for their beds, people in general had to get by with a skin or something similar. As for the insulation of the walls and roof, it was rather indifferent. The tightest were naturally buildings of turf, which was used in the coldest regions.

In Iceland skeletons have been examined from an early church-yard, and it has been discovered that the types correspond only in part to the Nordic ones. There is a palpably foreign element, which clearly comes from their Celtic fellow-immigrants, the Irish. We have in written sources much evidence of intermarriage. This must have been the case in the other Viking colonies too, where the colonists married either into the local population or those who—by compulsion or of their own free will—accompanied the Vikings on their journeys.

Clearly, it was the robust and energetic who went forth—the weaklings stayed safe at home. A burial ground in Jutland with well-preserved skeletons shows that a good many were infirm.

The basic factor for a healthy or sickly family is to some extent diet. This we know, where we have the remains of meals in culture-layers, traces of grain-growing, and the impressions or charred remains of rye, wheat, oats and barley. Quantities of bones show that animal-foods, meat and milk, played an essential part. We have seen how food was prepared over the fire—pots for soup were coming into use—or in roasting-pits, which were heated by red-hot stones, and which preserved the nutritive value. Cattle, sheep, goats, pigs and poultry were kept in varying numbers, and were frequently intended for slaughter. Horse they allowed themselves to eat only in extreme emergency (as also dogs), but this did not apply to a sacrificial feast. In that case it was a duty, if we dare believe the story about Hakon Adelstensfoster. Other meat and fish they got by hunting. They had nets and hooks to catch both fresh-water fish, such as salmon, and sea fish, cod, herring, etc. Whale and seal played no little part in their diet; in addition they used the skins.

Besides grain, which was ground to flour (bread and porridge) or used for beer, they must have had vegetable-foods, such as onions, and also fruit (apples, etc.). Together these provided an all-round diet, which would also cover vitamin needs. An interesting study has been made in Iceland on the basis of old Nordic sources, and although it relates to a somewhat later period than the Viking era, there is reason to take other points of view into consideration because of the strong continuity on the great island.

Vitamin A was obtained from fish, not least from the meat of whale and seal. Sea-birds, milk and butter, and animals slaughtered in the autumn (which was usual at the time), were likewise an important source. Well dried or salted, the foodstuffs retained their vitamin value throughout the winter.

Vitamin B was easily procured from the coarsely ground flour, but many of the other foods mentioned were also important for this.

Vitamin C was apparently a problem in a time that knew neither potatoes, nor lemons, nor many kinds of greenstuff. But it is probable that onions, which are mentioned in the runic inscriptions, and berries, meat and fish compensated for these. Scurvy is mentioned in later Icelandic writings, and this disease may have occurred, but clearly only in special situations, e.g. on long journeys by ship.

Vitamin D (lack of this causes rickets) is found in fish liver and fat fish, but milk and butter also contain vitamin D (as does other produce from grazing animals).

A common element in the Norsemen's food was the preponderance of meat, fish and dairy produce. In some places, e.g. in Denmark, bread and porridge were particularly important. Elsewhere, greater gains were to be had from bird-catching, seal-hunting, etc.

The diet was simple and nourishing. It required strong teeth. To judge from the worn-down state of their teeth, it seems as though the Vikings all but pulverized their food, and that it was at all events a more effective way than our present method. Without a healthy diet containing vitamins, the Norsemen would never have been able to carry out their remarkable expansion and develop such a lively intellectual activity.

It is in itself astounding that people all over the north felt the same

wanderlust and made their way far and wide, with an energy that has few parallels in history. Alongside the activity that was developing in foreign countries, the community at home was also beginning to take on the form it has in our own day. The farms lay gathered together or spread out in the same favourable places as in our time, some on the same sites. The towns were established from the points of view that apply also today: centrally for communications, preferably with harbour possibilities, or with a rich hinterland. Several towns were founded during the Viking era, and already acquired importance at that time. Even outside Scandinavia, the increase in urbanization can be set in conjunction with the extensive trade of the Vikings. London, Dublin and many other towns took a decisive step forwards.

It is hard to say what stamped the period most, the outward-directed activity, or the even rhythm of the farm, determined by rural industry and the seasons. And yet tradition and independence were striking the whole time, also in the arts. Foreign motifs and subjects were taken over, it is true, but the work of the best artists is completely original. Individual style asserts itself again and again, but also an impression from the nature of the country and the character of the people breaks through. One can be in no doubt about where a poem like *The Prophecy of Volvan* was created. Earthquakes, volcanoes and geysers are phenomena which one would be familiar with only in Iceland. At the same time, plants are mentioned which are not found in Iceland, in a misleading way, for example mistletoe, which is thought to be a tree.

The ways of life and the culture of the Viking era were more complex than one might at first suppose. They range over violent ravaging and a regular legal order, over an art of imagination, which was unsurpassed in its time, and more down-to-earth ideas for improving ship-building, rural industry and fishing. Voyages of discovery took Norsemen beyond the bounds of the known world, to Greenland and America. Conquests and emigration caused large numbers of the Norsemen to stay away for ever. When this energy-sated period came to a close, the united kingdoms fell apart. Others seized power outside the north. Christianity triumphed for good.

Nevertheless, traditions were not broken everywhere. The Nordic layers of the population made themselves felt, both politically and culturally. Social conditions in the Danelaw were stamped hence-forward by the strong Danish element. The language held its own for many generations in the Scottish islands.

Many other examples might be mentioned. One of the most interesting relics is the Isle of Man, between Ireland, England and Scotland. Here the Nordic quality has been preserved right down to our own time, although it has been exposed to gradual Anglicisation. Originally it was a Celtic population that lived on this isolated, quite fertile island, which is roughly $12\frac{1}{2} \times 25$ miles in size. An Irish dialect was spoken here, and the population had long since been Christianized.

When the Vikings turned up around the year 800, it was Norwegians from the north-east; later came Danes too. We see how the first to bury their dead laid them in Viking mounds. Later, the Norsemen intermarried with the original population and became Christian. This appears from the typical stone crosses, which have runic inscriptions in Norwegian and Nordic ornamentation. The first crosses were executed by a Viking whose name was Gaut. He discovered that the easily-worked slate-stone was reminiscent of wood, the Norsemen's favourite material for carvings. A series of quotations from the crosses reveal the development: Mael Brigde (a Celtic name) ordered a cross from the Viking Gaut; Thorleiv (Nordic) raised one in memory of Fiacc (Celtic); Driuian (Pictish), the son of Dugald (Celtic), was married to Athmhaoil (a Celtic woman) and received his memorial tribute in a Nordic runic inscription. It is clear that the Scandinavian language gradually came to prevail.

In keeping with this, Scandinavian motifs from mythology and the

The body of the Oseberg wagon rests on two decorated wooden supports which end in human heads. Two of them are naturalistic, so lifelike that one seems to see the Viking in front of one, with his open eyes; alertly he looks straight ahead. A man like the northerner of today, but not stamped with the same ideas. The other two faces are coarse caricatures. The mouths open into a mighty leer. They are a pair of men from whom one can expect anything, from a scathing retort to a blow of the axe.

later styles (especially Jelling and Mammen art) were often used on the crosses. There was clearly direct contact with the artist-craftsmen at home. Nordic trends of taste were followed abroad.

The island came under the dominion of the Vikings and for long held an independent position. In the middle of the island, which was divided according to Nordic custom into six areas (sheadings = *skeyr,* ship-laws), lay the Thing. The site consists of an artificial elevation, 3 metres high and 25 metres long, which is still called The Tynwald (Thing-field). Here laws for the island were adopted and here the other functions of the Thing were exercised. It preserved its character into our own century, and self-determining farmers used to meet round an inner circle of Thing-men. Later, British laws had to be adopted by the Tynwald in order to acquire validity.

Such was the vitality of the Norsemen's culture. The history of the Isle of Man reflects the Vikings' destiny, their journeys, their cultural and legal independence, and their traditions, such as they have been found, remaining in our own day. Here, what was created a thousand years ago survives and enriches our knowledge of the Vikings and the world in which they lived.

Bibliography

A very large and varied literature is available on the Viking era. Here it is only possible to draw attention to some of the more important books and interesting articles which provide supplementary information. Among the older publications, a number continue to be worth reading. J. J. A. Worsaae's account, *Minder om de Danske og Nordmændene i England, Skotland og Irland*, 1851, is a pioneering contribution on the basis of fresh observations. Johannes Steenstrup's four-volume work on the Vikings, *Normannerne*, 1876—82, constitutes an important collection of material, to which may be added the volume *Normandiets Historia under de syv første Hertuger*, 1925. The Norwegian scholar Alex. Bugge, equally able and equally independent, wrote *Vikingerne I-II*, 1904—06. A later account is T. D. Kendrick, *A History of the Vikings*, 1930.

Lively summaries have been produced by H. Arbman and M. Stenberger, *Vikingar i Västerled*, 1935, and H. Arbman, *Svear i Österviking*, 1955. Johs. Brøndsted's *Vikingerne*, 1960, has already attained a wide circulation and translation into several languages. Well illustrated and full of life is Palle Lauring, *Vikingerne*, 1956.

Interpretations of Viking life have been in sharp contrast to each other, both through individual points of view and through a certain national cast in the respective Nordic countries, as well as in the foreign countries to which the Norsemen made their way. However, these differences are being evened out, thanks to the scientific attitude which now prevails as against the relics from early days. A number of problems which seem incapable of solution (e.g. the question of Rollo's nationality—Danish or Norwegian—about which the sources hand down contradictory information) have been pushed to one side as being of less consequence in relation to the cultural picture itself and its decisive features. Yet much remains to be done, including many more excavations, in order to widen and deepen our knowledge of Viking culture.

One of the courses now adopted, which has proved effective against national prejudice, amongst other things, is collaboration between scholars from different countries (excavations in Iceland, publication of source-material, and also books written by scholars from several countries to throw light on a subject). In addition, scholars from different fields of science (e.g. historians, archaeologists and philologists) regularly get together at conferences, *Vikingkongresser*, where relevant topics are discussed.

Expansion to the west:
H. Shetelig, *Vikingeminner i Vest-Europa*, 1933.
J. Adigard des Gautries, *Les noms de personnes scandinaves en Normandie*, 1954.
A. W. Brøgger, *Ancient Emigrants*, 1929.
J. Brøndsted, *Northmen in North America before Columbus*, 1954.
H. Ingstad, *Västervägen till Vinland*, Stockholm, 1965.
G. Jones, *The Norse Atlantic Saga*, 1964.

Jarlshof: J. R. C. Hamilton, *Excavation at Jarlshof, Shetland*, Edinburgh, 1956.
The Northern Isles, ed. by F. T. Wainwright, 1964.
Viking Antiquities in Great Britain and Ireland, ed. by H. Shetelig, I—VI, Oslo, 1940—54.
Sv. Marstrander, *Viking*, 1962, p. 123 (the Setnes find).
On Iceland: *Forntida i Island*, ed. by M. Stenberger, Copenhagen, 1943.
On Ireland: M. and L. de Paor, *Early Christian Ireland*, 1958.
On Greenland a large number of monographs are available in *Meddelelser om Grønland* (Brattahlid, Gardar, Herjolfsnes, P. Nørlund in No. 76, 1930; 88, 1934).
Recent literature and points of view: P. H. Sawyer, *The Age of the Vikings*, London, 1962.

Expansion to the south and east:
Latest contributions to the discussion in *Atti del VI Congresse internazionale delle scienze preist. e protoist.*, Rome, 1962, I, p. 221 (H. Arbman) and III, p. 175 (Artsikhovski).
T. J. Arne, *La Suède et l'Orient*, Stockholm, 1914.
W. Raudonikas, *Die Normannen der Wikingerzeit und das Ladogagebiet*, Stockholm, 1930.
K. O. Falk, *Dnjeprforsarnes namn i Konst. Porfyr. De adm. imperio*, Lund, 1951.
A. Stender-Petersen, *Varangica*, Århus, 1963.

Early finds of Scandinavian-Slavonic origin:
H. Arbman, *Meddelanden från Lunds hist. mus.*, 1959, p. 110.
M. Stenberger, *Tor*, 1959, p. 192.
A. Kirpitsjnikov, *Sovjetskaja arkhelogija*, 1961: 4, p. 178; 1965:3, p. 196.

Particular historical or runological sources:
L. Jacobsen, *Svenskevældets fald*, Copenhagen, 1929.
Vilh. La Cour, *Danevirkestudier*, Copenhagen, 1951.
L. Jacobsen and E. Moltke, *Danmarks Runeindskrifter*, Copenhagen, 1942. *Norges Runeinnskrifter med de yngre runer I ff.*, Oslo, 1944 ff.
S. B. F. Jansson, *Runinskrifter i Sverige*, 1943.
The Novgorod finds, see Artsikhovski in *Atti del VI congr. Staraja Ladoga*, Kuml., 1958, p. 117 and 133; 1960, p. 135 and 137.

The Arab sources and the most important of the Byzantine:
H. Birkeland, *Nordens historie i middelalderen efter arabiske kilder*, Oslo, 1954.
Constantine Porfyrogennitus De administrando imperio, ed. by Gy. Moravcsik and R. J. H. Jenkins, Budapest, 1949.

Coins:
M. Dolley, *Viking Coins of the Danelaw and of Dublin*, The British Museum, London, 1965.
Br. Malmer, *Nordiska mynt före år 1000*, Bonn-Lund, 1966. Cp. the above-mentioned book by P. H. Sawyer.

Ships:
A. W. Brøgger and H. Shetelig, *Vikingeskipene*, Oslo, 1950.
B. Almgren, *Tor*, 1962, 1963.

Monographs:
Finds of treasure:
S. Grieg, *Vikingetidens skattefund*, Oslo, 1929.
R. Skovmand, *De danske Skattefund*, Aarb. f. nord. Oldkyndighet, 1942.
M. Stenberger, *Die Schatzfunde Gotlands* I-II, 1947—58.

Town-finds:
H. Arbman, *Birka I-II, Die Gräber*, Stockholm 1940—43, Birka, 1939.
H. Jankuhn, *Haithabu, ein Handelsplatz der Wikingerzeit*, Neum., 1956.

Various kinds of early find:
S. Grieg, *Gjermundbufunnet*, Oslo, 1947.
J. Petersen, *De norske vikingesverd*, Oslo, 1919; *Vikingetidens smykker*, Stav., 1928; *Vikingetidens redskaper*, 1951.
D. Selling, *Wikingerzeitliche und frühmittelalterliche Keramik*, Stockholm, 1955.

Important grave-finds:
Osebergfunnet I-IV, Oslo, 1917—28, by A. W. Brøgger, Hj. Falk, S. Grieg and H. Shetelig.
N. Nicolaysen, *Langskibet fra Gokstad*, Christiania, 1882.
E. Dyggve, *Jelling*, Nationalmuseet, Copenhagen, 1961.
K. Thorvildsen, *Ladby-Skipet*, Copenhagen, 1957.
Th. Ramskou, *Lindholm Høje*, Nationalmuseet, Copenhagen, 1960.

Fortifications:
P. Nørlund, *Trelleborg*, from the report of the National Museum, 1949.
O. Olsen, *Skalk*, 1965, 4, p. 18.

Art:
O. Klindt-Jensen and D. Wilson, *Viking Art*, 1966.

Religion and mythology:
A. Bæksted, *Guder og helte i Norden*, Copenhagen, 1963.
E. O. G. Turville-Petre, *Myth and Religion of the North*, London, 1964.
O. Olsen, *Hørg, hov og kirke*, Copenhagen, 1966.

Visits to the memorials of the Viking era:
Med arkæologen Danmark rundt, Politikens Forlag, Copenhagen, 1963.
Med arkeologen Sverige runt, Forum, Stockholm, 1965.
Reiserfører til fortiden. Med arkeologen rundt Oslofjorden, J. W. Cappelens forlag, Oslo, 1966.

Index

Page references to pictures are followed by a 'P', references to maps by an 'M'.